A Modern Jew In Search Of Soul

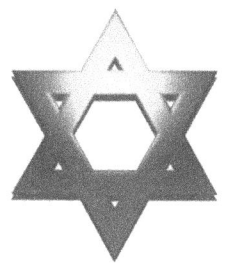

Some Other Titles From New Falcon Publications

Aha! The Sevenfold Mystery of the Ineffable Love — **Aleister Crowley**
Bio-Etheric Healing — **Trudy Lanitis**
Undoing Yourself With Energized Meditation and Other Devices
Secrets of Western Tantra: The Sexuality of the Middle Path
Dogma Daze — **Christopher S. Hyatt, Ph.D.**
Rebels & Devils: The Psychology of Liberation **Edited by Christopher S. Hyatt, Ph.D.**
Aleister Crowley's Illustrated Goetia
Taboo: Sex, Religion & Magick
Sex Magic, Tantra & Tarot: The Way of the Secret Lover
  Christopher S. Hyatt, Ph.D., and Lon Milo DuQuette
Pacts With The Devil
Urban Voodoo: A Beginner's Guide to Afro-Caribbean Magic
  Jason Black and Christopher S. Hyatt, Ph.D.
The Psychopath's Bible — **Christopher S. Hyatt, Ph.D., and Jack Willis**
Ask Baba Lon — **Lon Milo DuQuette**
Aleister Crowley and the Treasure House of Images **J.F.C. Fuller, Aleister Crowley,**
  Lon Milo DuQuette and Nancy Wasserman
Enochian World of Aleister Crowley — **Lon Milo DuQuette and Aleister Crowley**

Info-Psychology   Neuropolitique   The Game of Life
What Does WoMan Want? — **Timothy Leary, Ph.D.**

Be Yourself - A Guide to Relaxation and Health
Dr. Israel Regardie's Definitive Work on Aleister Crowley, The Eye In The Triangle
Healing Energy, Prayer and Relaxation
My Rosicrucian Adventure
Teachers of Fulfillment
The Complete Golden Dawn System of Magic
The Eye in the Triangle: An Interpretation of Aleister Crowley
The Golden Dawn Audio CDs
The Legend of Aleister Crowley
The Portable Complete Golden Dawn System of Magic
The Tree of Life
What You Should Know About the Golden Dawn — **Dr. Israel Regardie**

Roll Away The Stone/The Herb Dangerous — **Dr. Israel Regardie and Aleister Crowley**

Rebellion, Revolution and Religiousness — **Osho**
Reichian Therapy: A Practical Guide for Home Use — **Dr. Jack Willis**
Woman's Orgasm: A Guide to Sexual Satisfaction — **Benjamin Graber, M.D.,**
  and Georgia Kline-Graber, R.N.
Shaping Formless Fire   Seizing Power   Taking Power — **Stephen Mace**
The Illuminati Conspiracy: The Sapiens System — **Donald Holmes, M.D.**
The Secret Inner Order Rituals of the Golden Dawn — **Pat Zalewski**
Sufism, Islam and Jungian Psychology — **J. Marvin Spiegelman, Ph.D.**
Nonlocal Nature: The Eight Circuits of Consciousness — **James A. Heffernan**
on What is — **Ja Wallin**

MANY OF OUR TITLES AVAILABLE ON KINDLE!
Please visit our website at http://www.newfalcon.com

Other Titles by Dr. Israel Regardie

A Garden of Pomegranates
A Practical Guide to Geomantic Divination - A Small Gem
Attract and Use Healing Energy - A Small Gem
Be Yourself - A Guide to Relaxation and Health
Ceremonial Magic
Dr. Israel Regardie's Definitive Work on Aleister Crowley,
 The Eye In The Triangle
Healing Energy, Prayer and Relaxation
How To Make and Use Talismans - A Small Gem
My Rosicrucian Adventure
Teachers of Fulfillment
The Art and Meaning of Magic - A Small Gem
The Body-Mind Connection, A Path to Well-Being - A Small Gem
The Complete Golden Dawn System of Magic
The Complete Golden Dawn System of Magic Book 1 - Ltd. Edition
The Complete Golden Dawn System of Magic Book 2 - Ltd. Edition
The Complete Golden Dawn System of Magic - The Black Edition
The Eye in the Triangle: An Interpretation of Aleister Crowley
The Golden Dawn Audio CDs, Vol. 1, Vol. 2, and Vol. 3
The Legend of Aleister Crowley
The Magic of Israel Regardie
The Middle Pillar
The Philosopher's Stone
The Portable Complete Golden Dawn System of Magic
The Tree of Life
The Wisdom of Israel Regardie - Vol. I
 Selected Introductions, Prefaces and Forewords
The Wisdom of Israel Regardie - Vol. II
 Selected Essays and Commentaries
The Wisdom of Israel Regardie - Vol. III
 Selected Articles, Introductions, Prefaces and Forewords
What You Should Know About the Golden Dawn
Aha! (Dr. Israel Regardie and Aleister Crowley)
Roll Away The Stone/The Herb Dangerous
 (Dr. Israel Regardie and Aleister Crowley)

MANY OF OUR TITLES AVAILABLE ON KINDLE!
Please visit our website at http://www.newfalcon.com

Copyright © 2020 Michael Miller

All rights reserved. No part of this book,
in part or in whole, may be reproduced, transmitted,
or utilized, in any form or by any means, electronic or mechanical,
including photocopying, recording, or by any information storage
and retrieval system, without permission in writing
from the publisher, except for brief quotations
in critical articles, books and reviews.

ISBN 13: 978-1-56184-572-9
ISBN 10: 1-56184-572-8

First Edition 1986
Second Revised Edition 2020

The paper used in this publication meets the minimum requirements
of the American National Standard for Permanence of
Paper for Printed Library Materials Z39.48-1984

Printed in USA

NEW FALCON PUBLICATIONS
2046 Hillhurst Ave., Room 23
Los Angeles, CA 90027
www.newfalcon.com
email: info@newfalcon.com

A Modern Jew
In Search Of Soul

Edited by Michael Miller, Ph.D., M.Ed., M.S.
and Delfina Marquez-Noe

Foreword by William A. Cohen, Major General USAF, Ret; Ph.D.
Introduction by Mary L. Marquez

NEW FALCON PUBLICATIONS
LOS ANGELES, CALIFORNIA

Dedication

This book is dedicated to the Memory of
Bertha Miller, My Loving Grandmother
who showered me with her deep
unconditional love.

Michael Miller, Ph.D., M.Ed., M.S.

Preface

It is with great pleasure that we present *A Modern Jew in Search of Soul*. After countless hours of reading and rereading the essays that fill these pages, we feel confident that it will take you on a thought provoking journey, and you will be inspired as well.

It isn't enough to have deep philosophical conversations, and to think about our search for soul, but to live it. Our power lies in putting those principles to work and to take actions that have impact in the world today, because life is sacred.

Ultimately, our desire to feel our connection to God through our search for soul is ineffable.

Michael Miller, Ph.D., M.Ed., M.S.
Delfina Marquez-Noe
2020

Contributing Authors

William Alex, M.D.

Rabbi Jack Bemporad, D.D.

Robert Bosnack, J.D.

Yishoel ben Baruch ha Chassid

William A. Cohen, Major General USAF, Ret; Ph.D.

Gustav Driefuss, Ph.D.

Rabbi Ted Falcon, Ph.D.

Helen Janiger

James Kirsch, M.D.

Mary Louise Marquez, B.A.

Rabbi Levi Meier, Ph.D.

Bertha Miller

Martin Mondrus, M.F.A.

Gloria Orenstein, Ph.D.

Robert Rosen, M.D.

J. Marvin Spiegelman, Ph.D.

Daryl Temkin

Arthur Waskow

Clara Zilberstein, Ph.D.

Foreword
William A. Cohen, Major General USAF, Ret; Ph.D.

It's been thirty-five years since the first edition of *A Modern Jew in Search of Soul* was published in 1986. Much has happened since then. We face new issues and our continued search for soul. These new issues are introduced within. My contribution is included in the new edition, which involves my own personal search. Although I am much older than I was in 1986, I still consider myself a modern Jew.

I was asked to do this foreword not because I best understand the challenges and potential solutions explored by more traditional highly qualified, and sometimes passionate Jewish authors, but because of my background. I claim neither expertise nor full familiarization with the sacred traditions of our faith.

Even as a modern Jew, no doubt I bring a different perspective shared by few others. I come from a background that will be unfamiliar to many readers. Granted, I possess some familiar Jewish heritage. I am a Cohen by birth. I am well-educated with a Ph.D., from a well-known California university. I have lived in and even fought for Israel. I am a former graduate school president, and have written books published in many languages including Hebrew in Israel and Arabic in Middle Eastern countries.

But in other ways as a Jew I am significantly different, even seriously lacking, as I grew up, was not encouraged to study Torah and I never had a Bar Mitzvah. Few of my neighbors were Jewish. I didn't know the simplest of prayers until I attended the United States Military Academy at West Point. My perspective as a modern Jew, such as it is, comes from almost forty years in the military profession, flying in the Air Forces in combat of both the United States and Israel.

My well-known Ph.D., professor, Peter Drucker, "the father of modern management" probably had the greatest Jewish influence on me. Peter, who was born a Jew, was raised by Jewish parents. Even so, he was raised as a Christian in turn-of-the-century-Austria prior to Hitler coming into power.

Once asked in class by a student how he acquired such broad knowledge and experience as to be able to solve the difficult problems in many different industries and countries which puzzled and confounded the kings, presidents, and corporate heads who consulted him, he answered without hesitation: "I never bring my knowledge or experience to any situation; rather, I bring my ignorance and lack of experience."

Peter Drucker, like Rambam in the 12th century who struggled to reconcile science with his faith in providing solutions for the Jews perplexed in the "modern times" of 1186, dared to write against the majority and in 1936 published a manuscript in his native German, "The Jewish Question In Germany." In that manuscript, he challenged the Nazis in their methods, theories and philosophy and proudly proclaimed his Jewish origins in the first paragraph. The manuscript was, of course, burned by the Nazis. By then he had already fled Germany for England shortly after Hitler came to power. In England he mastered English sufficiently to write a best-selling book on the rise of fascism which was reviewed favorably by one Winston Churchill. He showed others how to search for soul in the Jewish way by asking questions and having his clients themselves come up with the best answers, meanwhile freely admitting his own ignorance. This, I suggest, is what we, the searchers must do today. We must proceed not so much with our perfect knowledge, but raise and examine the questions which cause us to continue the search for soul.

An excerpt from the 1986 foreword:

The editors are pleased to present these variegated contributions to the most charged and poignant theme, when the past has seen the Jewish people utterly devastated by a Holocaust and reborn with the state of Israel. The essays, we are glad to say, are Jewish but not provincial. They speak of their own search for soul in personal and heartfelt ways. Among the writers are several rabbis, for example, orthodox, conservative, reform and even, as one described himself, "rebellious." There are psychologists and physicians, Jungian Analysts and professors, artists and writers, as well as other community members. Although our contributors are mostly American, we have included several people with long experience in Israel and Europe.

One might add that these days–which are often called "postmodern"–are filled with the opposite experiences of "return" to Jewish observance, along with fears of assimilation in the west and annihilation in the Middle East. In this context, these contributions are both thoughtful and heartfelt. They should help us all understand our fellow Jews and be more tolerant of the way each of us copes with the strains of continuing our heritage in the modern world while maintaining individuality.

We hope that our offerings will be received as a form of Jewish "ecumenism" and, therefore, help to bridge the gaps among ourselves as we hope to reach out to the world as well.

Introduction

Mary L. Marquez, B.A.

A Modern Jew in Search of Soul is a compilation of a unique rainbow of three perspectives in search of soul and Jewish wisdom. The three spectrums of this *rainbow* comprise beauty, intensity, and scholarship, and a variety of ways to explore, encounter and appreciate "soul," and if we are so fortunate, gain some wisdom in finding meaning to our lives, not just as Jews, but as human beings participating and contributing to the present community of man.

The three spectrums of **Part I**: *God and Man*, **Part 2**: *Thought and Judaism* and **Part 3**: *Reflections and Manifestations* are all intertwined. There is no real separation where soul and wisdom abide.

The first spectrum, **Part I**: *God and Man* encompasses rabbinical viewpoints which present and explore a variety of ways of search for soul: meditation methods using words, verses and prayers, a specific study of Job from the Bible, the study of man's "duality" of the Spirit and flesh, and the Jewish Mystical Movement of Chassidism, the search for divine intimacy:

> "Listening eagerly to the singing of the birds, the youthful Baal Shem came to understand and love their song. He learned of life from the secret whisperings of the leaves touched by gentle breezes, from the hum of the bee in quest of honey, and from the quiet, sensitive steps of the deer. In all the manifestations of Nature he saw the terror and the splendour of God, too. The terrific thunderstorm of

mid-Continent, the vivid lightening, the rushing of the river, the cheery burbling of the stream as through meadow and vale it wound its way, and the awe of the snowclad peaks of the mountains—all these contributed an indelible impression which was seared into his very soul."

The second spectrum of this "rainbow", **Part 2**: *Thought and Judaism* presents the thinking aspect (specifically, Jungian Psychology and Therapy) in search for soul. These individual scholars present how "psyche" as manifested by individual events or experiences, acknowledge and integrate their "faith" with their secular lives. Some of them discuss in depth, the relationship between early childhood Judaic education or lack thereof, due to assimilation into society at large and its impact on their personal lives. It is a fascinating insight into "soul" due to the variety of experiences of these Jungian scholars, some of which "return" to Judaism via their interpretation of some of their dreams and "psychic" events. "Jung, following the alchemists, called soul *Anima Media Natura*. The *Soul* in the *Middle* between opposing *Natures*. She is the medium, the conductor of both light and darkness, bond between formless eternal light and the darkness of earth and the underworld."

The third spectrum, **Part 3**: *Reflections and Manifestations-Life Variations to Soul*, is a prime spectrum of mothers, writers and authors, editors, rabbis, military, artists, teachers, professors, counsellors, physicians, and psychologists, and sometimes combinations of the same, who express their specific journeys or experiences to soul in the uniqueness of their lives. It is certain that whatever affiliation each person has had or has to Judaism, be it Orthodox, Reform, Conservative, Reconstructionist or Chassidism, or *other*, that the very search and exploration of soul can lead to realizations to one's own essence and wisdom. There is no "one" way to find one's numinosity in a world that is ever changing because each person is unique and ever changing. Where are we expected to begin the search for soul if it isn't from ourselves and others who are and have been and continue to be on a similar journey?

In summary, reader, *A Modern Jew in Search for Soul*, is one "*rainbow*" illuminating the way in the search for soul and wisdom. We are humans, but we are "beings" as well. We are not just bodies, but much more than that. We are already integrated. Our soul is us. When we abdicate the ego of who we think we are, we are capable of experiencing our true and higher selves.

Table of Contents

Preface by Michael Miller, Ph.D., M.Ed., M.S. — vii
    and Delfina Marquez-Noe
Foreword by William A. Cohen, Major General USAF, Ret; Ph.D. — ix
Introduction by Mary L. Marquez — xiii

PART I   GOD AND MAN:
The Wisdom of Judaism

Jewish Paths Toward Awakening — 1
    by Rabbi Theodore G. Falcon, Ph.D.
Job — 25
    by Rabbi Jack Bemporad
The Modern Jewish Man's Search for his Soul — 41
    by Rabbi Levi Meier, Ph.D.
A Jewish Mystical Movement — 53
    by Yisroel Ben Baruch Ha Chassid

PART 2   THOUGHT AND JUDAISM:
The Wisdom of the Psyche

In Search of One's Missing Soul — 71
    by Daryl Dovid Temkin
Judaism & Jungian Psychology: A Personal Experience — 81
    by J. Marvin Spiegelman, Ph.D.
Echad — 101
    by Robert E. Bosnak, J.D.
The Search of a Swiss Jewish Israeli — 105
    by Gustav Dreifuss, Ph.D.
An American in Jerusalem and the Search for Soul — 111
    by William Alex, M.D.
Reflections at Age Eighty Four — 127
    by James Kirsch, M.D.

Table of Contents Continued

PART 3 REFLECTIONS AND MANIFESTATIONS:
Life Variations to Soul

Jewish Pictures	141
by Martin Mondrus	
Editorial comment by J. Marvin Spiegelman, Ph.D.	
The Way of the Orthodox	157
by Robert A. Rosen, M.D.	
A Child Raised in Orthodoxy	175
by Clara F. Zilberstein, Ph.D.	
God's Gift to Me	179
by Bertha Miller	
Gender Politics and the Soul	181
by Gloria Feman Orenstein, Ph.D.	
How I Learned Judaism at West Point	205
by William A. Cohen, Major General USAF, Ret; Ph.D.	
Good Morning God	215
by Helen Janiger	
One Soul's Journey	221
by Mary L. Marquez	
Tikuum Olam:	
Repair of the World - Adornment of the Mystery	231
by Arthur Waskow	
Appendix I - Biographical Notes	241

Part One

GOD AND MAN:
The Wisdom of Judaism

*"the Lord God formed man from dust
of the earth. He blew into his nostrils
the breath of life, and man
became a living being."*
–Torah, Genesis 2.7

Illustration by Martin Mondrus

Jewish Paths Toward Awakening

Rabbi Theodore G. Falcon, Ph.D.

For this commandment which I command you today is not too wondrous for you, neither is it distant from you. It is not in the heavens that one would say, 'Who shall ascend to the heavens and get it for us that we might hear it and do it?' And that commandment is not beyond the sea, that you need say, 'Who will go across the sea to bring it to us so that we might hear it and keep it?'

Because the word is very near to you already, in your mouth and in your heart, for you to do. (Deuteronomy 30:11-14)

"It is proper to say before prayer, I hereby take it upon myself to fulfill the commandment: 'You shall love your neighbor as yourself.'" (From the Siddur Tehillat Hashem, prayerbook following the arrangements of Rabbi Isaac Luria and according to the text of Rabbi Shneur Zalman of Liadi. The Biblical reference is Leviticus 19:18)

Love is the Way to God.
Love is the Way of God.
Listen to the word of Love
Within your heart.

When I received the announcement for the twentieth anniversary reunion of my high school graduation (once I got over the realization that it was no mistake) one of the question on the sheet caught my attention. It asked "What was the most important thing you have learned since your graduation?"

I never went across country for that reunion, and, in fact, I did not return the questionnaire. But I thought about it for a long time.

The most important thing I have learned in those twenty years is that the world operates in a way somewhat different than I had been taught. I learned, both in my secular as well as my religious education, that in order to change the world it was necessary to get out there and protest, rally and shout. And in order to change the way things felt inside, it was also necessary to get out there and change the situations in which a life was lived.

Now I know that is, at best, half the story. I strongly suspect it is less than half. In order to affect my life it is necessary to change the nature of my consciousness. Otherwise, no matter what changes I make in the outside world, I will find myself winding up at the same place I began. And in order to truly change the world outside, it is also necessary to change the world inside. If such inner changes are not made, the outer ones gradually fade away and old problems reassert themselves. Again and again.

The basic problem then became: What is the best way to change the nature of my consciousness? If so much of my own life, and even the life outside myself, are supported by my own awareness, how can I control that awareness?

And that has been my search. It led me, first, away from the Jewish path I had learned, even in rabbinic school, into studying the Eastern traditions of meditation and Western traditions involving hallucinogenics and psychotherapies. Then it led to a reawakening of my own identity as a Jew, and a growing appreciation for the depths of spiritual teaching and tradition within the Jewish continuum. I am not talking about the spiritual teaching that is more a matter of words than of content. I am talking about serious meditative traditions that aimed to support the awareness of the One. For centuries, often unappreciated and unheard, there were teachers striving to fulfill the ancient visions of prophets and priests.

The path is filled with paradox. There is tradition, yet awakening is always new. There are techniques, yet meditation is always of the moment. What impresses me within the Jewish continuum is the ever-present battle against idolatry, whether that idolatry is represented outside or inside tradition itself. In the relatively few moments I have been offered of those timeless spaces of Realization beyond words and images, I understand that each of us must find our own Way. Judaism is a Path of many ways toward the One. We Jews have much in common, yet there is always that which is about to become part of the tradition which Moses already received at Sinai.

This is the wonder of the Jewish Path.

To listen to the heart is risky business. The deeper intuitions of our beings may often run contrary to the messages of our outer teachers. As we try to translate those inner yearnings we often stumble, find words with difficulty, appear less secure than others would have us be. What are we to do? Listen to parents, teachers, and other community representatives? Discover what is expected of us that we might expect the expected of those around us? And… somewhere along the way, begin to lose our awareness of that finer voice that spoke once from the heart?

If being Jewish involves reconnecting again with our deepest inner messages, then such a way of being is risky indeed. It would not be easy to be Jewish. It could run counter to our conditioning, it could demand new responses that have not yet been heard.

Such a Judaism would demand from many of us that same response that Abraham, as prototype of us all, acted out: a leaving of the familiar and a venturing out into the unfolding of an inner integrity.

> **And the Eternal said to Abram, 'Get yourself out from your country, from the place of your birth, and from your father's house, and go to the land which I shall show you.' (Genesis 12:1)**

The challenge to be a Jew is no different today, and the stakes no less significant. It would be easier to pretend otherwise.

But the spiritual search is no idle intellectual exercise. Those to whom the inner word speaks, understand that it is the evolution of the universe which needs the energies of the human being and human consciousness. When this being is stifled, and this consciousness clouded, the energies blocked within the individual are reflected in blockage outside. The universe provides a mirror reflecting our own condition, and we reflect it in return. If there is One God, then that Oneness connects all that is, and in the One each cell impacts the whole.

Spiritual awakening is one of the ways humans have discovered to hear again the Heart to all existence. Ultimately, the challenge to be a Jew is to awaken to the true nature of our Identity in this One.

Every true spiritual tradition offers its followers both general and specific instructions to help them on the path to enlightenment. Such enlightenment, or illumination, comes through experiences of awakening, in which the ordinary is transcended and the fuller vision of unitive reality achieved. This article focuses on the Jewish experience of awakening, and on the specific metaphors of Jewish perceptions of enlightenment. The emphasis here is on the personal and the experiential. In the course of the following pages, specific ways will be offered to encourage the reader to approach experiences directly. The Jewish texts considered will not be the esoteric but the ordinary. It is in the midst of the everyday that enlightenment hides most creatively.

It is peculiar that we seldom know we have been asleep until we awaken. It is difficult to know the nature of our further awakening to spiritual levels of reality until we have in fact awakened.

One might imagine living in a village set at the foot of a large mountain. After occupying ourselves with village activities, we may become curious about the mountain itself, and begin to climb.

Soon we can look down and perceive our village from a totally new vantage point. In the arrangements of the streets, we understand relationships that had been hidden from us before. It is the same village, but our awareness of it has shifted.

Still further up the mountain we begin to see a flow of vehicles and people traveling from home to work and school in the morning and back again in the evening. Deeper rhythms of village life can be appreciated the higher up we climb. And what we learn about the mountain itself cannot be known from the village below.

The village is the place in which we all live, the village of our physical being. From that physical reality, the mountain of consciousness rises. Each true spiritual tradition is represented by a path up that mountain. The closer we are to the ground, the further apart each tradition appears. In fact, it sometimes is difficult to image that we are climbing the same mountain at all. But as we progress upward, the paths begin to converge, and we can appreciate each other along our individual ways. At the summit there is only One.

It often seems as though the Jewish path is far more oriented toward helping us live in our village reality than urging our climb up the mountain of consciousness. Certainly, we as Jews have always been concerned with issues of social justice, but what about the specifically spiritual dimensions of our lives? There are at least two reasons why the Jewish tradition of meditation, of mysticism, and of enlightenment have tended to be hidden from us.

The first speaks to an essential paradox in all religious traditions. On the one hand, a religion is designed to offer its adherent steps toward awakening. But awakening can seem frightening, it means leaving the securities of the known village realities. So religious have tended also to provide the individual protection from the immediacy of the spiritual encounter. That protection is in the form of external authority. Enlightenment is awakening to internal authority. Sometimes the authority protects the people from what it perceives would overwhelm them, and at other times it responds to fears the people themselves voice. Perhaps authority often supports itself by encouraging the fears of others.

Standing at Sinai is one metaphor in Jewish tradition for the process of enlightenment. In that story, we were afraid:

> **And all the people perceived the thunderings, and the lightnings, and the voice of the horn, and the mountain smoking; and when the people saw it, they trembled, and stood afar off. And they said to Moses, "You speak to us, and we will hear; but let not God speak to us, lest we die."**
>
> **And Moses said to the people, "Fear not, for God is come to prove you, and that His fear may be before you, that you sin not."**
>
> **But the people stood afar off, and Moses drew near to the thick darkness where God was. (Exodus 20:15-18)**

There is thick darkness to be encountered in the spiritual search. There are moments of fear, of awe. Such exist whenever we release our hold on current beliefs about the nature of our reality. Yet within the darkness is unequalled Light.

Secondly, the specifically spiritual in Judaism has been neglected because we are today products of the Enlightenment, the Nineteenth Century movement which was more an enlightenment of intellect than of spirit. We are heirs to the belief that with science all things are possible. Only recently has this scientific distrust of spiritual teachings been questioned. With the emergence of the new physics we are finally living in an age where intellect and spirit may point to the same view of Ultimate Reality. The arrogance of both may now be softening to allow mutual support and validation.

Although enlightenment is outside of our ordinary view of reality, it is not an unnatural state of being. Perhaps it is the most natural, since it represents a stripping away of the limitations created through a sole focus on our physical growing on this planet. Those limitations are necessary to our individual biological survival and evolution, and are most clearly represented in that structure of consciousness we call the ego. The ego allows us to operate as a separate organism in the world, learning to take care of ourselves and develop many of the talents and skills which help us to create for ourselves the qualities of life we desire.

Yet it is crucial to recognize that the ego is not the only identity which we have. Other structures of consciousness must come into play for the expanded perceptions of unity and oneness that mark the spiritual path. The ego helps us deal with the village; it is not alone adequate for climbing the mountain. When one attempts that climb with ego, the result is conceptualization and power-tripping. Such attempts are often marked by beliefs to be defended, argued, and urged on others. When other people accept those beliefs, we feel more secure in them ourselves. But we can never be secure enough.

The quality of knowing through a non-ego identity, we can call "faith." Unlike an ego belief, such faith does not support attempts to disprove another's way and replace it with one's own. The knowing is deeper, less open to the need to defend and attack. The Hebrew work for this kind of knowing is *emunah*, which refers to an established reality. The experience of *emunah* is a spiritual kind of perception.

Spiritual learning is different from all those kinds of learning. Other learning comes to us from the outside in. We read, we listen, and then we repeat. We may combine things in our own ways, but we are repeating that which has come to us from the outside. We find the expert teacher or text and learn from them what we wish to know. Although this is frequently the way we strive to awaken spirituality, the nature of the awakening demands a different focus. Spiritual learning always comes from the inside out, not from the outside in. There is already within our own consciousness all that we seek. We are already within our own consciousness all that we seek. We are already the answer that we yearn for. What is required is the awakening of the consciousness which sleeps within us.

Different traditions have created various metaphors with which to describe the nature of that which is awakened. Even as we enter into the metaphors, it is important to trust our own individual experience and to proceed with intellectual and psychological honesty.

In seeking Wisdom, the first stage is silence, the second listening, the third remembrance, the fourth practicing, the fifth teaching. (Solomon ibn Gabirol; Spain, 11th century)

The first step in perceiving beyond the limitations of our ego state of consciousness is allowing silence. Stress-reduction through relaxation processes and meditation helps us enter the kind of silence in which we can remember deeper aspects of our own being.

Relaxation, which creates an environment of silence, is crucial for spiritual unfoldment. Our tensions physically, emotionally, and mentally keep us in a state of relative contraction from which fuller dimensions of the universe cannot be realized. Many have experienced spontaneous awakenings, occasioned by accident, emergency, or reverie, but the conscious path to such explorations is best begun with the release of stress. The fears which can arise from the explorations of new territories are also calmed through relaxation. Fear is the great mind-killer, the great limiter, and entrance into the inner realms of silence is eased as our fears are eased. Relaxation is the great fear-soother.

Relaxation practices are probably meditations in themselves, and function well as preparations for deeper work. The three most basic methods of relaxation focus on the breath, the body, and the use of sensory imagery. The secret of the breath is that an extended exhalation relaxes. The muscles, first tightened and then relaxed, help the entire system to release excess stress. Imaging ourselves at a peaceful, secure setting can be effectively relaxing.

After relaxing, it is possible to enter into the inner silence in ways deeper than before. In that silence it is possible to hear more deeply. In that silence one meets oneself.

The release of stress is the first step toward the inner silence from which listening can take place beyond the usual noise of limited consciousness. Meditation is the next step into that silence.

MEDITATION

In Hebrew, the word for meditation is *hitbodedut* which literally means "being alone with one's self." It is usually a withdrawal from outer focus to inner focus, a moving away from the external clamor and clutter. When the prophet Elijah, seeing confirmation of his way, entered a cave on Mount Horeb, this metaphor for *hitbodedut* is offered us:

> **And behold, the Lord passed by and a great and strong wind rent the mountains, and broke in pieces the rocks before the Lord; but the Lord was not in the wind; and after the wind an earthquake; but the Lord was not in the earthquake; and after the earthquake a fire; but the Lord was not in the fire; and after the fire a still small voice. (I Kings 19:11-12)**

Meditation is one of the most direct ways to make ourselves available for that still small voice, that sound that springs from the inner silence.

Jewish traditions of meditation are extensive. From the early schools which focused on the images of Ezekiel through Abulafia in the thirteenth century who taught permutations of the Hebrew alphabet; from the Essene contemplative communities to the conversations with God taught by Nachman of Bratzlav there is incredible richness and variety.

Teachers of meditation in Safed in the sixteenth century offered verses from the Bible to serve as meditational phrases, to be repeated silently. Sometimes these verses were chosen to teach specific spiritual lessons, in which case students would receive other verses when they had awakened to the wisdom hidden within their phrase. Sometimes these verses were focuses which were used continuously, in a fashion which today would be called a *mantra*, a Sanskrit word which means "*a sound that frees*."

A simple Jewish meditation uses the word *shalom* as a focus. Begin a period of meditation with some moments of relaxation, letting go of whatever tension you can. Then begin to hear the word *shalom* repeating in your mind. Attend to the word as it repeats slowly. When other thoughts and images come into the mind, gently release them, and return your attention to shalom. Like many of the Jewish forms of *hitbodedut*, the use of this word is both extremely simple as well as effective.

The central meditational phrase of Jewish tradition is called the *shema*, and deserves much exploration.

THE SHEMA
SHEMA YISRAEL
ADONAI ELOHEYNU
ADONAI ECHAD

LISTEN, ISRAEL:
THE ETERNAL IS OUR GOD
THE ETERNAL IS ONE.

These six words are found in Deuteronomy 6:4 and are together referred to as the *shema*, the Watchword of Jewish faith. The *Shema* is the central phrase of Jewish spiritual unfoldment. Most of us are familiar with an older translation: "Hear, O Israel, the Lord our God, The Lord is One." These words are beyond simple translation. It is necessary to meet them on deeper and deeper levels.

There is an ancient mystical tradition that there are seventy secret Names of God. The word *shema* has been separated to read *shem ayin*, which means "the Name" and the number 70. "With such synchronicities does the significance of the *shema* impress itself upon us. In the lettering of the *shema* in every Torah scroll, the last letter of the first word and the last letter of the last word are written larger than the other letters. The two letters, read together, spell *ayd* which means "witness." The *shema* is not simply an intellectual affirmation. It is the basic response to that affirmation of One. It directs us toward a way of being in the world. A way of living as a witness to the One. It is necessary to consider the worlds of the *shema* in some greater depth.

SHEMA, YISRAEL

Listen, Israel! It is command, call, challenge, and promise, all in one. And who is "Israel?" Israel is the name given to Jacob after he wrestles with the angel;

> **And Jacob was left alone; and there wrestled a man with him until the breaking of the day. And when he saw that he prevailed not against him, he touched the hollow of his thigh; and the hollow of Jacob's thigh was strained, as he wrestled with him. And he said, "Let me go, for the day breaks." And he said, "I will not let thee go, unless you bless me." And he said to him, "What is your name?" And he said, "Jacob." And he said, "Your name shall no longer be called 'Jacob,' but 'Israel,' for you have striven with God and with men, and you have prevailed." And Jacob asked him, "Tell me your name." But he said, "Why do you ask about my name?" And he blessed him there. And Jacob called that place Peniel, "for I have seen God face to face and my life is preserved." And the sun rose over him as he passed over Peniel, and he limped upon his thigh. (Genesis 32: 25-32)**

Israel is the name given to Jacob after he wrestles with the angel. His sons, among whom are the leaders of the twelve tribes, are called the children of Israel. Through them our people get this name. But the heart of the name comes from the drama of the wrestling. Israel means one who strives for God, one who stands for God. Within each of us is that part which stands for God, and it is to this part that the *Shema* speaks most clearly.

It is interesting that in the Torah Jacob is sometimes called "Jacob" even following that story. Sometimes Jacob and sometimes Israel. Sometimes trying to be something he is not and sometimes standing for God and being simply who he is. That is how it is with us. We awaken, and then we fall into sleep once again. To receive enlightenment does not mean that from that point on in our lives we constantly live enlightenment. We sleep again. Yet we are different. Like Jacob, we carry a limp with us into the world. Having opened to the infinite, we are somehow the same and never the same.

LISTEN, ISRAEL!

There is within each of us the consciousness which was first called Israel in our ancestor Jacob. Yet we each must awaken to it in our own way, just as Jacob had to. It is not possible to do it another's way because that was their way. That does not mean that there is nothing is common about our ways. There is. But ultimately the awakening emerges within us, the learning comes from the inside flowing outward. It comes in response to the Word we hear and recognize within ourselves. Awakening is a transaction between inside and outside.

ADONAI ELOHEYNU
THE ETERNAL ONE IS OUR GOD

Adonai is the word which is read instead of the four-letter Name of God indicated by the Hebrew letters yod-hay-vav-hay. This four-letter name, called the tetragrammaton, is not to be pronounced. What was once whispered in the ancient Temple by the High Priest in the Holy of Holies on the Day of Atonement is not to be spoken aloud. It is beyond speaking. It is a word which is beyond word.

The letters themselves reflect the Hebrew word for "being," past, present, and future. That which Is.

The Name cannot be spoken because it is too big to be spoken. Perhaps shouted, perhaps chanted, because the shout and the chant do not end so quickly. This is Hebrew speaking the One "What is." Perhaps the sound of the Name is hidden in the silence.

ADONAI ELOHEYNU
THIS 'WHAT IS' THIS ETERNAL ONE, IS OUR GOD

The word usually translates into English as "God" is *Elohim*, and *Eloheynu* is *Elohim* with a possessive suffix meaning "our." In Hebrew, the -im ending is a plural ending for a noun. Literally, this word would mean "Gods," or "our Gods," but it has always been translated as a singular noun, and takes a singular form of a verb. It is a Unity acting like a multiplicity. It is a One acting like a many.

Elohim is the presence of God within each one of us. And this *Elohim* is of *Adonai*: The Eternal One is our God. One might translate, The Eternal One is God in us.

ADONAI ECHAD

ALL THAT IS IS ONE
THAT WHICH IS ETERNAL IS ONE.

Here is the Shema. It has been a watchword of this faith for a very long time. It is waiting always for us to hear.

SHEMA YISRAEL
ADONAI ELOHEYNU
ADONAI ECHAD

LISTEN, ISRAEL:
THE ETERNAL IS OUR GOD
THE ETERNAL IS ONE.

BEGINNING MEDITATION WITH THE SHEMA

The words are to be carried upon the heart, waiting for the heart to open and receive them. The words are to be carried gently, lovingly, that we may receive them when we open. We receive them with our mind, our intellect, and we await the opening of the heart. We await the deeper realization.

One kind of meditation is literally a gentle and loving carrying of words like these silently within the mind. Practice reciting the shema until the words become truly comfortable. Then you are ready to use the Shema as a meditation.

Begin a Meditation Journal in which to record your experiences. This kind of journal can be extremely supportive to your journey, and can help you perceive more clearly your own process and progress. Remember to date each entry. The Journal is private, and everyone deserves to have private territory no matter with how many others we live.

At the beginning, leave your journal open during your meditations. When you conclude, jot down any particularly strong thoughts or perceptions. Note any changes you experience in your meditation. Progress in meditational practice is not linear, but your journal entries can give you a broader view of your progress than otherwise is possible. Any resistances that arise deserve careful attention as well, and the Meditation Journal is ideal for that.

Then be with the words. And listen…

In the inner silence, let the Shema repeat gently. Word by word, phrase by phrase. Over and over again. There is a holy vibration to these words which has supported spiritual unfoldment for so many generations.

When the mind gets caught on other thoughts, gently bring the Shema back. You might later note what thoughts were most pervasive, most intrusive. Focus on the six words of the Shema. Let the words repeat so you hear them inside. If a melody comes, let it be. If the images of the letters come, let that be. And focus on the Shema.

This inner listening with the words calling us to listen is extremely powerful. Like any meditation, it is a practice that takes some time.

It is helpful at the beginning to create space to bring the Shema into meditative consciousness in morning and evening. There are the initial instructions which immediately follow the Shema in Torah, to focus on these words when we lie down and when we rise up.

We are also told to be with these words when we walk on the way and when we sit in our house. Lying down, rising, being outside of our home and being inside of our homes–these circumscribe our entire existence. Ultimately, we are instructed to keep the Shema in mind and in heart all the time. We are to be ever mindful of the One reality we are. This is the essence of the Jewish Path.

Mediation is one of the most profound ways of centering ourselves when we become upset and unclear. Yet we cannot suddenly begin a meditation program at such different times. Only the meditation that has already become a part of our lives can help in an emergency.

Tradition says that we are to repeat the Shema at the time of death. At the moment when the ego meets its most feared enemy, we are to recite the Word of One. Yet how can we expect ourselves to be able to do so unless that Shema has already become a part of ourselves? The mindful always. And that, of course, is the goal.

It is not easy to remember. We become involved in the urgencies of our daily lives, we collapse into the drama of our personal lives, we are involved in the activities of the world at large. How simple it is to forget the deeper rhythms which flow through that inner silence.

Many of us hold a belief in one God which in fact makes no difference in the way we experience our lives. It may be an intellectual concept, a philosophical principle, a matter of right thinking, perhaps even right preaching. But along the paths of Jewish meditation, much deeper appreciations of the wonders of Oneness begins to open. This is nothing outside it. Each of us in a location of consciousness, a point of awareness. What is unique about us is our particular location, our point of view. What we share is consciousness, since we are each aspects of the One Consciousness, the One Awareness, the One Who Is. To awaken to this identity is a life-shaking event. We become Israel.

This realization awakens within our own consciousness. Jewish tradition gives us that which can be used to support our awakening, but no tradition can give it to us from the outside. No teacher, no master, no text can do for us what we must do for ourselves. They serve as reminders, as records of those who have travelled their paths before, as challenges. With each of our own steps we are writing new chapters in what is now the unfolding oral tradition of Jewish meditation.

We relax and enter into the silence. We listen and we remember. What we perceive out of the silence strikes us with an immediacy, a "realness" unequalled by other kinds of perceptions. Yet afterward, except for the excitement, the words are often not so new-sounding. The specific realities were already "known," they just were not "realized."

Love is like that. We can talk about it, read about it, write about it, and "understand" it. Yet when it awakens for us, it is always something "new." The realization of Love is always more than the conceptualization. Sometimes the words we use after such a realization are not that different, yet we hear them on a deeper level. This is the way it is with spiritual realizations. The words make most sense after the experience. We cannot know we have not truly had the realization until after we've had it.

After we've had it, and have talked about it, the immediacy of the realization tends to diminish. After first we might hardly notice it, since the experience is living so vividly in our words. But something is different. The immediacy is lost. Realization is not a one-time event. It is a space consciousness to be approached again that we might actualize the fullness of our humanity.

THE SABBATH

Our world does not ordinarily support such realizations because of the demands and expectations of our usual roles. Tradition gives us cycles of rituals and symbols with which to aid our remembering. All true rituals are externalizations of inner reality. Our rituals and symbols are meant to function as reminders of the One Who we are.

Rituals and holy days follow a calendar and so are signals of spiritual rhythms which may or may not be actualized at the time of the observance. They are reminders of the deeper realities from which we are separated only as a consequence of our own state of consciousness. So each ritual, essentially, offers us an invitation to again realize Spirit. Each ritual is an invitation to a holy time.

The most important ritual time of Jewish tradition is the Sabbath, celebrated from Friday evening to Saturday evening each week. The *Shabbat* is the celebration of creation and the celebration of freedom. Both in one. It is a time of spiritual rest and nourishment. It is a moment of completeness and wholeness. All this and more. Whether we can realized *Shabbat* during the calendar time dedicated to it or not, Shabbat is a reality which can infuse our days with ultimate meaning. Without *Shabbat* we are empty wanderers of an alien planet. *Shabbat* is the celebration of meaning, and its symbols are particularly powerful.

The welcoming of the Sabbath, the *Kabbalat Shabbat*, includes blessing of light, wine, and bread which corresponds to the three levels of soul identified in the *Zohar*. The *Zohar* is the central text of the Jewish mystical tradition, appearing in the thirteenth century in Spain. The light awakens the *neshamah*, the highest level of Spirit which is given us to support the full realization of *shabbat*. The wine speaks to the fullness of the heart, the soul level called *ruach*. The bread is the symbol of nourishment for the *nefesh*, the animal soul with which we experience the physical world of the senses.

THE LIGHT: NESHAMAH

This three-dimensional entry into Shabbat is meant to invoke fuller levels of awareness, since the Shabbat itself represents the transcendence of the ordinary. The Light which reflect energies of *neshamah* is no ordinary light. It is the reflection in the outer world of the light in consciousness. It is a symbol of the Light of Illumination, the Light which banishes the shadows and carries understanding and knowledge. It is the Light of Spirit. So we are not merely commanded to kindle candles in the outer world. We are called upon to remember Light, to make it real within our awareness, to invite its influence, and then to express it through the candles of Shabbat.

Prior to lighting your candles, reach for silence. Close your eyes and let go for a moment. If you have already been practicing Jewish meditation, focus on your meditational phrase for a few moments. And then allow Light to appear. It may come as an inner image of a candle, of a spark, of a ray of light. Allow it to appear as it will. And then honor it with your attention. Breathe it into your body, and let it flow through every cell. Let that Light bring its peacefulness, its wholeness, into every part of your body. Imagine that Light making clear that which is muddled in your life. Imagine sharing the Light with the world, with all humankind. And when that peacefulness begins to flow through you, open your eyes and kindle the Shabbat candles. Bring that Light outside and celebrate it there.

BARUCH ATAH ADONAI
ELOHEYNU MELECH HA-OLAM
V'TZIVANU L'HADLIK NER SHEL SHABBAT

Blessed Are You, Eternal One,
Our God Who Is Ruler of the World
Who sanctifies us with ways called Mitzvot
And gives us this Mitzvah of kindling Sabbath Light.

Imagine that Jews everywhere are bringing Light into their awareness, and supporting in that way the evolution of Light and Love in the entire world. Tradition says that on the day all Jews celebrate Shabbat, Messiah will come. And it is probably so.

Messiah is not a person, it is a level of awareness. The Messiah is within each of us. One might imagine that on the day the Messiah comes, the call will go out: "Will the *real* Messiah please stand up." When the Messiah has truly come, all of us will rise. The Messiah appears on the day that is total Shabbat, when consciousness knows its Source. Perhaps, like the hundredth monkey phenomenon, we Jews have enough energy to change the world with our Shabbat. We will not change it with any rote observance, but with the Shabbat of the Spirit, the confluences of *nefesh, ruach*, and *neshamah*. In such a way will we connect heaven and earth.

THE WINE: RUACH

The place where heaven and earth meet is symbolized by the heart. It is the energetic meaning of the Jewish star in which energies from below and energies from above meet in perfect balance. The triangle pointing upward represents earth energies, the material world reaching its influence upward, seeking spiritualization. In Jewish tradition, this lower is often seen as the *Schechinah*, the female aspect of God, the immanence of God in the world, that which is receptive to the energies coming from above.

The *ruach* is the level of soul, at the heart space, that looks down at the *nefesh* and up to the *neshamah*. It is the soul, the identity, that connects the upper and lower realities. One might identify the *neshamah* with full mental states, the *ruach* with complete emotional states, and the *nefesh* with secure physical states. One might say that the content of *neshamah* is the awareness of One, of *ruach* the love of One, and the content of nefesh the possible physical expressions of Oneness. On an emotional level, the feeling of One is always Love. This does not mean romantic love, although it is certainly a part of Love. This fuller Love is an attitude toward self and the world. It is an experience of acceptance, of compassion and of openness.

Jewish tradition is too seldom recognized as a tradition of Love today, largely because of Christianity's use of the term. Most of us grow up either believing or countering the notion that Christianity is the religion of Love and Judaism one of Law. It is time to speak again of Love and Judaism without apology. The words which immediately follow the *Shema* in the Torah announce the consequence of the realization of the One: "Then you shall love the Eternal One your God..." (Deuteronomy 6:5). Love always follows true spiritual awareness. This has been the lesson of every master in every tradition. The problem has to do with finding the proper way of bringing that Love into right expression in the world.

The Light symbolized by the *Shabbat* candles brings energy down into the heart where it is experienced as Love. And the wine is the symbol of that fullness of heart.

The wine carries the light into the heart, and so it is the second of the blessings of *Kabbalat Shabbat*, the welcoming of the Sabbath.

> BARUCH ATAH ADONAI
> ELOHEYNU MELECH HA-OLAM
> BORAY P'REE HA-GAFEN
>
> Blessed Are You, Eternal One,
> Our God Who Is Ruler of the World
> Creator of the fruit of the vine.

Following the blessing, the wine is tasted, drawing into self the nourishment of the ruach.

THE BREAD: NEFESH

The bread symbolizes an earth supportive of our physical needs. Our *nefesh* our sense-based, self, sees the light and tastes the wine transmitting energies from above, and awaits the bread that nourishes from below. The traditional *shabbat* bread is the *challah*, bread from the choicest of flours. It is customary to bless two loaves, symbolizing the double portion of *manna* received prior to *shabbat* in the ancient wilderness.

The *nefesh*, symbolized by our ego identity, is so fragile in the world. Our days are numbered, our futures unknown. The *challah* speaks the essential wholeness of nefesh, the certainty, the solidity, when in touch with the soul influences of ruach and spirit energies of *neshamah*.

Hold the bread for a moment before the blessing. Feel its reality. Understand that it represents earth nourishing your body. Everything that you need is provided. That is the body's Shabbat experience. All the senses are gratified. All is as it is supposed to be. We are exactly where we want to be, doing what we want to be doing, being who we are wanting to be. That is the *shabbat* of the *nefesh*. And the bread is its symbol.

BARUCH ATAH ADONAI
ELOHEYNU MELECH HA-OLAM
HA-MOTZEE LECHEM MIN HA-ARETZ

Blessed Are You, Eternal One,
Our God Who Is Ruler of the World
Who brings forth bread from the earth.

After the blessing, take a piece of the bread and allow yourself to truly taste it. Share pieces with those others present with you. Enjoy the tastes of Shabbat.

To celebrate is to remember, on some level, that which we are.

It is to bring some ray of light, some taste of sweetness, some sense of nourishment into our world. The weekly ritual of *Kabbalat Shabbat* calls us on a regular basis to the deeper energies of which we are a part. Every nowhere, when seen from a different perspective, becomes a "now here," just as every moment of the ordinary, when seen from a higher viewpoint, is already holy ground.

DEEPER INTO A BLESSING

The blessings themselves deserve some attention. Every Jewish blessing contains both the universal as well as the particular truth to which it is directed. At every step, Jewish tradition calls to those who will hear. Listen.

BARUCH ATAH ADONAI
ELOHEYNU MELECH HA-OLAM

Blessed Are You, Eternal One,
Our God Who Is Ruler of the World.

So begins just about every Jewish blessing. It is the statement of the Universal preceding the specific focus of that blessing.

To bless is, in fact, a daring event. It means to open ourselves to an awareness that is bigger than our normal consciousness. It means letting go of the judgements with which we normally perceive the world. To bless is to acknowledge, however dimly, the absolute wonder of all that is. The absolute perfection of All That Is. The Hebrew word, *baruch*, which implies "kneeling," as if this attitude is a surrender to What Is. To open in blessing, to at least speak an awareness that All That Is, is blessed. Perhaps the voiced blessing will become a real blessing. Perhaps our words will attract the awareness.

Blessed are You, Eternal One. It is the *nefesh* turning its eyes upward beyond itself, speaking the perfection of Being of which it is a part. And then: **Our God, Ruler of the world.** *Adonai*, the All beyond words, is again linked to *Eloheynu*, the manifestations of that Allness within our own consciousness. This *Eloheynu* is **Our God**, is the **ruler of the world**. This manifestation within us carries the energies that shape this part of the universe, this part of the whole. The Eternal One is reflected within each of us as our God, and within us this energy is active to influence the reality in which we live.

To bless is to make holy piece of our reality. To bless is to make a connection between above and below, between the world within and the world without. To bless is to announce the Divine within the daily. In our world, this itself is a thing of wonder.

The beginning of each blessing restates the heart of Jewish faith, and then the words proceed to specify the action in the world into which this heart is to be celebrated.

One blessing which supports growth through some of the most difficult of times is called the *Shehechiyanu*. Tradition instructs us to recite it whenever we do something for the first time. We are always if we are paying attention, doing things for the first time. The world is always new.

BARUCH ATAH ADONAI, ELOHEYNU MELECH,
HA-OLAM SHEHECHIYANU, V'KI'MANU, V'HIGIYANU
LAZMAN HA-ZEH

You are Blessed, Eternal One,
Our God Who rules the World,
Who keeps us in Life always.
Who supports the unfolding of our uniqueness
And Who brings us to this very point.

We are here with purpose. Our lives have meaning. And we are that meaning and that purpose. We are the actions of God on earth. We are the being of God on earth. This is the beginning of Jewish spirituality. All else is commentary. Let the unfolding happen within you, and then go and read what others have written about their journey. Enjoy the metaphors and the stories. Learn from them that others may learn from you.

Be silent. Listen. Hear. Then act. And teach.

It is time.

JOB

By Rabbi Jack Bemporad

The Book of Job is universally recognized as one of the great literary and religious pieces of all literature. The book is a poetic drama. It begins with a prose prologue (chapters 1 and 2), continues through 3 cycles of speeches between Job and his three friends, Eliphaz, Bildad and Zophar (Chapter 3-31); Elihu's speech (Chapters 32-37), God's interrogation and Job's response (Chapters 38-42:6) and it closes with an epilogue (Chapter 42:7 to the end).

There is considerable controversy as to how genuine the various parts of the book are. Some scholars believe that the only genuine features of the book are the cycles of speeches as well as God's interrogation and Job's response. These scholars maintain that the Prologue and Epilogue, as well as Chapter 28, Elihu's speech and much of the divine speech are later addenda. These scholars take an extreme view. Most scholars grant that the prologue and the epilogue (with the exception of Chapter 42: 12-16) are original parts of the book, and most scholars reject Chapter 28, Elihu's speech and the references to Behemoth (Chapter 40: 15-24) and Leviathan (Chapter 41: 1-end) as later interpolations.

The Prologue (Chapters 1 and 2) sets the stage for the problem of the book. Job is "blameless and upright" a man who "fears God and turns away from evil". He is exceedingly prosperous and blessed in full measure in every way. When the "sons of God" present themselves before the Lord and Satan (who is here simply the accuser), "Have you considered my servant Job, that there is none like him on the earth, a blameless and upright man who fears God and turns away from evil." Satan responds to God's question by saying, why shouldn't Job be righteous since God has blessed him in everything. But if God were to face him with adversity, God would see that Job would turn against God and curse him.

God then places Job in Satan's power and in one fell swoop, all save his wife, who Satan saves as an ally (Chapter 2:9) is immediately taken from him. His children, his property and his servants were destroyed. Job, far from cursing God, proclaims "naked I came from mother's womb and naked shall I return; the Lord gave, and the Lord has taken away; blessed be the name of the Lord." (Chapter 1:21) Again Satan appears before God; again God speaks of his servant who is unique in his righteousness. Satan claims that "all that a man has he will give for his life, but put forth his hand now and touch his bone and flesh and he will curse thee to thy face." God puts Job into Satan's power; only his life must be spared. Job is afflicted with sores all over his body and is in intense pain. His wife pleads with him to curse God and thus die, Job maintains his faith and asks–Shall we receive good at the hand of God and not evil? and "in all this Job did not sin with his lips". The issue at stake between God and Satan is–Is there such a thing as virtue for its own sake? Will Job remain virtuous when the rewards of virtue are not praise and prosperity, but irreparable loss and intense suffering? The Prologue only introduces the issue and it informs the reader that Job is innocent and this his sufferings are in no sense deserved.

Job's three friends, Eliphaz, Bildad and Zophar hear of Job's affliction and come to visit him. While they see him from afar, he is so disfigured, they cannot recognize him. They week over his fate and sit with him for seven days and seven nights without a word. Finally, Job breaks the silence and initiates the conversation by cursing the day of his birth and longing for death.

Chapter 3:11 -13

Why did I not die at birth, come forth from the womb and expire? Why did the knees receive me? Or why the breasts, that I should suck? For then I should have lain down and been quiet; I should have slept; then I should have been at rest.

Chapter 3:16-19

Or why was I not as a hidden untimely birth, as infants that never see the light? There the wicked cease from troubling, and there the weary are at rest. There the prisoners are at ease together; they hear not the voice of the taskmaster. The small and the great are there, and the slave is free from his master.

Death is the leveler. All achieve equality in death. Job longs for death.

Chapter 3:20-21

Why is light given to him that is in misery, and life to the bitter in soul, who longs for death,...

Eliphaz responds to Job's lament. His discourse is well organized, coherent and well tempered. He states first that Job "instructed many" and..."strengthened the weak hands" when others were in trouble. "Your words have upheld him who was stumbling and you have made firm the feeble knees. But now it has come to you and you of God your confidence, and the integrity of your ways your hope?" Eliphaz exhorts Job not to make an exception of himself, but to heed the very advice he gave others in trouble; namely to trust in God, who will save him. Secondly, Eliphaz states, "Think now, who that was innocent ever perished? Or where were the upright cut off?" Does Job really believe that evil can afflict the innocent? This would mean that God is not just. On the contrary, Job himself knows very well that "those who plan iniquity and sow trouble reap the same" (Chapter 4:8). Thirdly, Eliphaz claims that in a vision at night the truth was revealed to him, "Can mortal man be righteous before God? Can a man be pure before his Maker? Even in his servants he puts no trust, and his angels he charges with error; how much more those who dwell in houses of clay," (Chapter 4:17 ff) That is, man is too puny to question God. Even the angels are imperfect, how much more so is man. Finally, Eliphaz maintains that God guides all things including natural phenomena according to justice and this is the foundation for man's hope.

> As for me, I would seek God, and to God would I commit my cause; who does great things and unsearchable, marvelous things without number; he gives rain upon the earth and sends waters upon the fields; he sets on high those who are lowly, and those who mourn are lifted to safety. He frustrates the devices of the crafty, so that their hands achieve no success. He takes the wise in their own craftiness; and the schemes of the wily are brought to a quick end. They meet with darkness in the daytime, grope at noonday as in the night. But he saves the fatherless from their mouth, the needy from the hand of the mighty. So the poor have hope, and injustice shuts her mouth. Behold, happy is the man whom God reproves; therefore despise not the chastening of the Almighty. For he wounds but he binds up; he smites, but his hands heal. He will deliver you from six troubles; in seven there shall no evil touch you. In famine he will redeem you from death, and in war from the power of the sword. You shall be hid from the scourge of the tongue, and shall not fear destruction when it comes. At destruction and famine you shall laugh, and shall not fear the beasts of the earth. For you shall be in league with the stones of the field, and the beasts of the field shall be at peace with you. You shall know that your tent is safe, and you shall inspect your fold and miss nothing. You shall know also that your descendants shall be many, and your offspring as the grass of the earth. You shall come to your grave in ripe old age, as a shock of grain comes up to the threshing floor in its season. Lo, this we have searched out; it is true. Hear, and know it for your good." (Chapter 5:8-27)

Eliphaz's speech is an overpowering theological display. What is more, he speaks to Job as a prophet stating a divine teaching. Everything that happens is due to God's justice; the wicked will be God, he will be saved from his suffering.

Job's response is that Eliphaz's speech is beside the point. First of all he does not need reproof but sympathy. They are not indeed friends.

He who withholds kindness from a friend forsakes the fear of the Almighty. My brethren are treacherous as a torrent bed, as freshets that pass away, which are dark with ice, and where the snow hides itself. (Chapter 6:14-17)

But the essence of Job's response is simple. Wherein has he done wrong? What is his sin? He states, "Teach me and I will be silent; make me understand how I have erred. How forceful are the honest words! But what does reproof from you reprove?" (Chapter 6:24-25)

Finally, it is easy for others to talk of hope and trust. Job asks, "What is my strength that I should wait…Is my strength the strength of stones or is my flesh bronze…? (Chapter 6:11-13)

Bildad the Shuhite now responds to Job bluntly, "Does God pervert justice? Or does the Almighty pervert the right? (Chapter 8:3) He also refers to the death of Job's children, "If your children have sinned against him, he has delivered them into the power of their transgression." (Chapter 8:4) Bildad argues, "God will not reject a blameless man but will reward you in the end." (Chapter 8:20a)

Job now raises a different issue which foreshadows the confrontation later on in the book. How can man contend with God? There is no match between man and God. How can man maintain his innocence against God? God can easily overpower him. Job states, "For he crushes me with a tempest, and multiplies my wounds without cause; he will not let me get my breath, but fills me with bitterness. If it is a contest of strength, behold him! If it is a matter of justice, who can summon him? Though I am innocent, my own mouth would condemn me; though I am blameless, he would prove me perverse." (Chapter 9:17-20) God cannot only overpower Job but He can persuade him against himself and in spite of himself. In spite of all this, Job maintains his blamelessness. However, since God has all the power on his side, Job knows that in spite of his innocence he "shall be condemned." (Chapter 9:29) He states,

> If I say, I will forget my complaint, I will put off my sad countenance, and be of good cheer, I become afraid of all my suffering, for I know thou wilt not hold me innocent. I shall be condemned; why then do I labor in vain? I wash myself with snow, and cleanse my hands with lye, yet thou wilt plunge me into a pit, and my own clothes will abhor me. For he is not a man, as I am, that I might answer him, that we should come to trial together. There is no umpire between us, who might lay his hand upon us both. Let him take his rod away from me, and let not dread of him terrify me. Then I would speak without fear of him, for I am not so in myself. (Chapter 9:27-35)

If either Job could find an umpire who could be objective with respect to his claim of innocence or if only God would not terrify him, then he could plead his case. If Job could plead his case before God, if only God would not terrify him and give him some respite from his suffering, then Job say to God:

> Do not condemn me; let me know why thou dost contend against me. Does it seem good to thee to oppress, to despise the work of thy hands and favor the designs of the wicked? Hast thou eyes of flesh? Dost thou see as man sees? Are thy days as the days of man, or thy years as man's years, that thou dost seek out my iniquity and search for my sin, although thou knowest that I am not guilty, and there is none to deliver out of thy hand? Thy hands fashioned and made me; and now thou dost turn about and destroy me. Remember that thou has made me of clay; and wilt thou turn me to dust again?" (Chapter 10:2-9)

Job now draw the logical conclusion from his innocence combined with his suffering. It must be that God:

> destroys both the blameless and the wicked. When disaster brings sudden death, he mocks at the calamity of the innocent. The earth is given into the hand of the wicked; he covers the faces of its judges–if it is not he, who then is it?" (Chapter 9:22-24)

Job has raised the question which his experience of excruciating suffering together with his recognition of his own innocence cannot help but bring to the fore. Namely, that there is no justice in the world; both the blameless and the wicked are destroyed.

Zophar the Na'amathite now joins the dialogue and states explicitly what the others only implied. He states, "For you say, 'My doctrine is pure, and I am clean in God's eyes,' But oh, that God would speak..." (Chapter 11:4-5a) What you would learn is that "God exacts of you less than your guilt deserves". (Chapter 11:6b) Zophar also argues that Job "set your heart aright" (Chapter 11:13) and thereby be secure. Job's responses become increasingly bitter. First he condemns the friends. They are at ease and all they can do is condemn those whom misfortune overtakes. (Chapter 12:5a) He tells them, "As for you, you whitewash with lies; worthless physicians are you all." (Chapter 13:4) What Job seeks is a confrontation with God. He states:

> **I would speak to the Almighty and I desire to argue my case with God (Chapter 13:3a)**
>
> **Let me have silence, and I will speak, and let come on me what may. I will take my flesh in my teeth, and put my life in my hand. Behold, he will slay me; I have no hope; yet I will defend my ways to his face. This will be my salvation, that a godless man shall not come before him. Listen carefully to my words, and let my declaration be in our ears. Behold, I have prepared my case; I know that I shall be vindicated. Who is there that will contend with me? For then I would be silent and die. Only grant two things to me, then I will not hide myself from thy face: withdraw thy hand far from me, and let not dread of thee terrify me. Then call, and I will answer; or let me speak and do thou reply to me...(Chapter 13: 13-22a)**

Job calls God to judgment as in a lawsuit. A lawsuit could be conducted by either asking a series of questions or by being asked a series of questions. Job is ready to take either side. "Call, and I will answer; or let me speak, and do thou reply to me." (Chapter 13:22)

Eliphaz is alarmed at Job's utterances. He accuses Job of forsaking his religion and indicates that his own words have condemned him.

> **But you are doing away with the fear of God..." (Chapter 15:4a)**
>
> **For your iniquity teaches your mouth, and you choose the tongue of the crafty. Your own mouth condemns you, and not I; your own lips testify against you." (Chapter 15:5-6)**
>
> **Why does your heart carry you away, and why do your eyes flash, that you turn your spirit against God, and let such words go out of your mouth? (Chapter 15:12 and 13)**

In opposition to the accusations of the friends, Job stands firm. They are "miserable comforters". (Chapter 16:2a) But God is his witness. He will vindicate him. (Chapter 16:19) Job knows that his "redeemer lives" (Chapter 19:25a)

> **For I know that my Redeemer lives, and as last he will stand upon the earth; and after my skin has been thus destroyed, then from my flesh I shall see God, whom I shall see on my side..." (Chapter 19:25-27a)**

Both Bildad and Zophar are disturbed at Job's rejection of justice in the world. Bildad claims that "the light of the wicked is put out" (Chapter 18:5) and Zophar asks Job, "Do you not know this from of old, since man was placed upon earth, that the exulting of the wicked is short, and the joy of the godless but for a moment?" (Chapter 20:4-5) (See especially Bildad's speech in Chapter 20.)

Job now directly confronts this oft repeated doctrine of the friends that the righteous prosper and the wicked perish. In the most explicit terms, he rejects it completely. He states,

When I think of it I am dismayed, and shuddering seizes my flesh. Why do the wicked live, reach old age, and grow mighty in power? Their children are established in their presence, and their offspring before their eyes. Their houses are safe from fear, and no rod of God upon them. Their bull breed without fail; their cow calves, and does not cast her calf. They send forth their little ones like a flock, and their children dance. They sing to the tambourine and the lyre, and rejoice to the sound of the pipe. They spend their days in prosperity, and in peace they go down to Sheol. They say to God, Depart from us! We do not desire the knowledge of the ways. What is the Almighty, that we should serve him? And what profit do we get if we pray to him? Behold, is not their prosperity in their hand? The counsel of the wicked is far from me. How often is it that the lamp of the wicked is put out? That their calamity comes upon them? That God distributes pains in his anger? That they are like straw before the wind, and like chaff that the storm carries away? You say, God stores up their iniquity for their sons. Let him recompense it to themselves, that they may know it. Let their own eyes see their destruction, let them drink of the wrath of the Almighty. For what do they care for their houses after them, when the number of their months is cut off? Will any teach God knowledge, seeing that he judges those that are on high? One dies in full prosperity, being wholly at ease and secure, his body full of fat and the marrow of his bones moist. Another dies in bitterness of soul, never having tasted of good. They lie down alike in the dust, and the worms cover them. Behold, I know your thought, and your schemes to wrong me. For you say, Where is the house of the prince? Where is the tent in which the wicked dwelt? Have you not asked those who travel the roads, and do you not accept their testimony that the wicked man is spared in the day of calamity, that he is rescued in the day of wrath? Who declares his way to his face, and who requites him for what he has done? When he is borne to the grave, watch is kept over his tomb. The clods of the valley are sweet to him; all men follow after him, and those who go before him are innumerable. How then will you comfort me with empty nothings? There is nothing left of your answers but falsehood. (Chapter 21:6-34)

Job defends his integrity and innocence, (Chapter 27:5-6) against the explicit attack of Eliphaz (Chapter 22:4ff) and the friends.

An impasse is reached with the friends. Now Job recounts the former times. The times when he was honored and God's care watched over him. These verses are some of the most beautiful and touching in the whole Bible. Job states, Oh that things were as of old,

> **when the Almighty was yet with me, when my children were about me; when my steps were washed with milk, and the rock poured out for me streams of oil! When I went out to the gate of the city, when I prepared my seat in the square, the young men saw me and withdrew, and the aged rose and stood; the princes refrained from talking, and laid their hand on their mouth; the voice of the nobles was hushed, and their tongue cleaved to the roof of their mouth. When the ear heard, it called me blessed, and when the eye saw, it approved; because I delivered the poor who cried, and the fatherless who had none to help him. The blessing of him who was about to perish came upon me, and I caused the widow's heart to sing for joy. I put on righteousness, and it clothed me; my justice was like a robe and a turban. I was eyes to the blind, and feet to the lame. I was a father to the poor, and I searched out the cause of him whom I did not know. I broke the fangs of the unrighteous, and made him drop his prey from his teeth. (Chapter 29:6-17)**

> **Men listened to me, and waited, and kept silence for my counsel. After I spoke they did not speak again, and my word dropped upon them. They waited for me as for the rain; and they opened their mouths as for the spring rain. I smiled on them when they had no confidence; and the light of my countenance they did not cast down. I chose their way, and sat as chief, and I dwelt like a king among the troops, like one who comforts mourners. (Chapter 29:21-25)**

But what a reversal, what a contrast between then and now. Job continues,

> **But now they make sport of me, men who are younger than I, whose fathers I would have disdained to set with the dogs of my flock. (Chapter 30:1)**

They abhor me, the keep aloof from me; Because God has loosed my cord and humbled me, they have cast off restraint in my presence. On my right hand the rabble rise, they drive me forth, they cast up against me their ways of destruction. They break up my path, they promote my calamity; no one restrains them. As through a wide breach they come; amid the crash they roll on. Terrors are turned upon me; my honor is pursued as by the wind, and my prosperity has passed away like a cloud. And now my soul is poured out within me; days of a affliction have taken hold of me. The night racks my bones, and the pain that gnaws me takes no rest. With violence it seizes my garment; it binds me about like the collar of my tunic. God has cast me into the mire, and I have become like dust and ashes. I cry to thee and thou dost not answer me; I stand, and thou dost not heed me. Thou has turned cruel to me; with the might of thy hand thou dost persecute me. Thou liftest me up on the wind, thou makest me ride on it, and thou tossest me about in the roar of the storm. Yea, I know that thou wilt bring me to death, and to the house appointed for the living. Yet does not one in a heap of ruins stretch out his hand, and in his disaster cry for help? Did not I weep for him whose day was hard? Was not my soul grieved for the poor? But when I looked for good, evil came; and when I waited for light, darkness came. My heart is in turmoil, and is never still; days of affliction come to meet me. I go about blackened, but not by the sun; I stand up in the assembly, and cry for help. I am a brother of jackals, and a companion of ostriches. My skin turns black and falls from me, and by bones burn with heat. My lyre is turned to mourning, and my pipe to the voice of those who weep. (Chapter 30:10-31).

If we were to summarize the arguments of Job and the friends to this point, we can see that the friends maintain the following:

First, God is just and thus no innocent person ever perished and no wicked person ever triumphed. Second, Job must have sinned. Otherwise, God would not be punishing him. The only alternative is that God is unjust and this would be blasphemy! Although at first it may seem otherwise, if one persists, he will discover that God's justice does indeed operate in this world as it does in all His doings in the natural and human realm.

Third, the Friends affirm that man is finite and of necessity imperfect and, therefore, is in no condition to challenge God or to question God's ways.

Job maintains, first of all, that he is innocent and even if God were to slay him, he would still defiantly proclaim his integrity. He states, "I will defend my ways to His face." Second, he challenges their basic proposition and maintains that often the wicked do prosper and the righteous do suffer and that God does not seem to hearken to the prayers of the oppressed. Third, he states that the Friends are white washers and liars and speak falsely for God but that God will vindicate him.

Two completely alien positions are expressed here. Implicit in the arguments of the Friends and the refrain that runs through all of their speeches is that justice is a fact and to deny it is to blaspheme God. They affirm that God's goodness completely depends on the actuality of rewards and punishment in this world. Job accuses them of lying (Chapter 13:4) and speaking deceitfully for God. He defends his integrity in the face of all.

Job can no longer converse with the Friends nor bewail his former glory and lament his degradation. Finally, he turns to God to vindicate him and to resolve his perplexity. Why do the good suffer? (And here we are aware that in Job's case it is the best man, the most righteous suffering the worst fate) (1:8, 11-12: 2:3-6) How do we reconcile the reality of the idea of justice with the fact of injustice? What is the role of God and man in all this? Job confronts God, as in a lawsuit, asking him to "call and I will answer or let me speak and do Thou reply to me" (13:22). God, however, is silent (19:7) and so Job asks in a crescendo of questions (31:5ff) "If I have walked with falsehood, if my step had turned aside from the way and my heart had gone after my eyes, my heart had been enticed by a woman." After vindicating his conduct with respect to personal morality, Job turns to his relationship with his fellow man. "If I have rejected the cause of my man servant; if I have withheld anything that the poor desired or have eaten my morsel alone;" "If I have seen anyone perish for lack of clothing." Now he turns to his own values and ideals: "If I made gold my trust...if I have rejoiced because my wealth was great;" "If I had rejoiced in the ruin of him that hated me."

The crescendo of questions addressed by Job to God plainly demonstrates his integrity and innocence. If he had done any of these then his punishment would be just but he is innocent and God is to declare to him wherein he had done wrong.

The Friends are left far behind. The can say nothing. Now it is God's turn. As in a lawsuit, God must either answer for Himself or pose questions for Job to answer. And finally God's voice issues forth from the whirlwind, "Where were you when I laid the foundations of the earth?" Who determined its measurements?" "Have you walked in the recesses of the deep?" "Have the gates of death been revealed to you?" "Who has cleft a channel for the torrents of rain... to bring rain in a land where no man is, on the desert where there is no man to satisfy the waste and desolate land." God begins by asking questions concerning the laws operating in nature. He then turns to the order of the animal world: "Can you hunt the prey for the lion and satisfy the appetite of the young lion?" "Who provides for the fallen prey?" "Who has left the wild ass go free?" Nature and animal life is so diversified and vast that the mere listing of these questions undercuts man's belief that the whole universe and everything in it functions for the sake of man and is created expressly for his needs. On the contrary, nature and animal life have their own laws which are separate and unrelated to man's needs. But even more, nature is indifferent to the morality so central to man. "The wings of the ostrich wave proudly but are they the pinions and plumage of love? She leaves her eggs on the ground forgetting that a foot may crush them...She deals cruelly with her young." "And the eagle, he spies out his prey and the young ones suck up blood." The brunt of these questions is to show overwhelming both the variety and diversity of existence and also its a-moral character. Nature and animal life do not function morally. The culmination comes when God confronts Job directly: "Will you condemn me that *you* may be justified... Deck yourself with majesty and dignity, clothe yourself with glory and splendor, look on everyone that is proud and abase him, look on everyone that is proud and bring him low and tread down the wicked where they stand? Hide them all in the dust together, bind their faces in the world below then will I also acknowledge to you *that your own right hand can give you victory*."

Job responds. He says he now understands and that he repents. What does Job now understand? What is God's answer? First, that man is not the center of the world. Second, that the order of the world is a-moral. Third, that God has placed upon *man* the task of "treading the wicked." Man must do the work on earth. *He* must realize that it is his "own hand that will give him victory." It is not up to God to do man's work. Fourth, that the world is unfinished and that man must strive to *become* for he is not *yet* its center. It is only in an unfinished universe, one that is in the making, one that is not won for God and man, that man can indeed have a task and a function. Yet, the good suffer and the best suffer most because it is the just and true and righteous that take upon themselves the task of bringing justice and truth in the world. When man has achieved his task, only then will a new heaven and a new earth appear together with a new heart and a new covenant, then the whole earth will be full of the knowledge of God and the lion will eat straw like the ox, then none shall be afraid, then God shall be one and His name shall be one.

In the Epilogue God announces that the Friends have not spoken correctly of God as Job has (Chapter 42:7-9), and therefore must offer up a burnt offering for their sins. What constitutes the Friends sin? The sin of the Friends is three-fold: First, they affirm that man indeed *is* at the center of the universe and thus assume that the natural and moral are one. In fact, as we have seen, Job's protest and the answer of God demonstrates that they are not in fact one but must be made one. Second, they deny the very nature of man's task. For them man has no self-transcending, nature transforming historical task. They thus deny what is at the heart of the prophetic concept of man that *he* is the instrument for the realization of the Messianic goal. Third, they make trivial the suffering and agony, the tragic pathos endured by the just man who is the agent for the realization of the good. The Friends want *God* to do *man's* work and thus they have not spoken correctly as Job who recognizes injustice yet sticks to his task and to his ideal despite the utmost agony and the most intense suffering. Job is the servant of God par excellence, and he symbolized to us the historic transformations that nature and man must accomplish if God's world is to emerge, to be brought into being.

Job is called the servant of the Lord and is symbolic of the suffering Israel who has a mission which can only involve suffering. The concept of the servant of God comes to completion in the heroic and terrifying servant passages in Second Isaiah. There God states "Hearken to me you who know righteousness, the people in whose heart is My law. Fear not the reproach of men." Israel the servant of God is to be a light unto the nations that God's salvation may reach to the ends of the earth. (Is. 49:6) In these servant passages the promise that was made to Abraham is transmuted into the broadest and most universal context. Now a law will go forth from God and His justice for a light unto the people. The servant of God is to carry God's law, he is to declare God's kingdom. His mouth is like a sharp sword (Chapter 49:2). He has the tongue of them that are taught (50:4). God's servant, Israel, must affirm God in the world, must bear witness undismayed to the ideal goal of brotherhood and peace.

The Modern Jewish Man's Search For His Soul

Rabbi Levi Meier, Ph.D.

I. God, Man and Halakhah (Jewish Law)

Jewish law is paradoxical but not contradictory in nature. The basis of the paradox is that God, the law-giver, has given His divine law to man who struggles to understand it with his human faculty and capacity (Heller, 5720). This union of divinity and humanity represents both the goal of the divine plan as well as an eternal conflict between different forces which encounter one another. A co-existence of opposite and different forces exist both in man and God. The Torah describes man as a finite being. Man is finite because he consists of two primary elements which represent man quo man. Man is God's spirit and human flesh (Genesis 6:3). Despite possessing God's spirit, man–precisely because of his uniqueness and quality–cannot live forever. God, also, has diametrically opposed qualities which characterize him, such as "He who creates peace and evil." (Isaiah 45:7).

It is understandable that Jewish Law and tradition, that link which relates the divine will to man, would contain the perplexing combination of divinity–humanity since each sphere in and of itself combines diverse and paradoxical motives. As previously explained, God creates peace and evil and humanity has both a divine spirit and human flesh. This analysis can be graphically described as:

DIVINITY
(peace and evil)

JEWISH LAW
(divine imperative which is understood by man)

HUMANITY
(divine spirit and human flesh)

How does man function in a universe which is composed of dialectics? Does he sway like a pendulum from one extreme to another until he achieves balance? More specifically, how does man accept the "rule of the Kingdom and heaven" when there is a perpetual struggle between God's spirit and human flesh? Should the flesh be sublimated constantly to the spirit? Is integration and wholeness sacrificed forever?

The antithetical nature of reality is seen as well in the abstract realm. Positive numbers co-exist with negative number and the laws of physics also demonstrates this principle.

Halakhah recognizes the duality of man's reality of spirit and flesh. Its laws allow for the expression of both forces, as long as they are directed to God. Every commandment, either positive or negative, requires *kavannah*–directional devoutness and piety toward divinity. In contrast to secular legal systems which emphasize the implementation of a behavior, Jewish law accentuates behavior combined with inner feeling, piety and the devoutness of the person. Even when flesh has its fulfillment through food, sex, dance or companionship, it is all God-directed.

Halakhah's recognition of man's duality does not alleviate the struggle between man's flesh and spirit. This challenge faces the existential man, and creates meaning for him.

II. The Nature of Religion

Within the framework of man's duality, theologians and scholars have always distinguished between religion in essence and religion in manifestation (Leeuw, 1933).

Twersky (1974) stated "that the dialectical relationship between religion in essence and religion in manifestation is at the core of the Jewish consciousness" (p. 69). *Halakhah*, Jewish law is the manifestation and concentration of a spiritual essence. *Halakhah* includes laws, religious institutions, and normative actions, while spirituality refers to moods, images, individual perceptions, and internal sensibilities. Manifestations and laws sometimes drift apart from essence and spirituality because a carefully constructed normative system cannot reflect fluid, spontaneous spiritual forces and motives.

Similar to Twersky (1974) but more universal in nature is Leeuw's (1933) thesis that religion consists primarily of essence and manifestation. He stated that reflection on the causes of natural phenomena cannot of itself constitute religion. It requires that the "object and subject are in a reciprocal operation." Man tried to elevate life, to enhance its value, to gain for it some deeper and wider meaning.

This balance between essence and manifestation has not always been maintained. James (1902) and Otto (1923) stressed the experiential aspects of religion, while Soloveitchick (1944) emphasized the implementation of the divine Law as the highest form of religious service.

James (1902) distinguished between institutional and personal religion. Institutional religion includes theology, ritual ceremonies, and ecclesiastical organizations. Personal religion refers to man's inner dispositions, his conscience, his feeling of helplessness, and the heart-to-heart, soul-to-soul relationship between man and his Maker. Religion cannot stand for any single principle–it is a collective name for religious fear, love, awe, joy, and other elements. James defined religion as: "feelings, acts, and experiences of individual men in their solitude, so far as they apprehend themselves to stand in relation to whomever they may consider the divine" (p. 31). The common man's perception of religion refers to life. The concern of religion is with the manner of our acceptance of the universe. Religion is with the in any case is necessary, i.e. dependence upon sheer mercy.

The supreme good is when we harmoniously adjust ourselves to unseen order. Within the religious sphere, articulated explanations are cogent only when they confirm pre-existing feelings and beliefs.

For some, the religion of healthy-mindedness leads to serenity, moral poise, and happiness. Feeling is a deeper source of religion than philosophic or theological statements, which are secondary products. A "science of religion presupposes immediate experiences as their subject matter. Philosophy only corroborates our pre-existent particularities" (James, 1902, p. 24).

Otto, (1923) likewise accentuated the essence of religion by emphasizing its numinous and other nonrational aspects. He stated that since expositions of religious truth are in language, these statement inevitably tend to stress the rational attributes of God. He coined the concept of the numinous–the aspect of deity which transcends comprehension in rational or ethical terms. The rational and moral are essential parts of what we mean by holy or sacred, only they are not the whole of it; nonrational elements are present as well. The holy, as a religious concept, is ineffable and it eludes definition. The numinous also involves a feeling of total dependence. This is an emotion of a creature that is overwhelmed by its own nothingness. This numinous feeling leads one to a vision of God as a *mysterium tremendum*. This view is similar to the religious view of primitive man. Primitive man viewed God with dread, as an awful, majestic presence and therefore God was totally unapproachable. Man is conscious of a *wholly other* that evades precise formulation in words. This nonrational aspect, in contrast to insight, is awakened by impulse, instinct, and the obscure forces of the subconscious.

In contrast to James (1902) and Otto (1923), Soloveitchick (1944) viewed the spiritual and religious as synonymous with the man of the law. Each lifetime reality is approached by the *halakhic* man in an *a priori* fashion. For example, the setting of the sun signals the time for evening prayers, and the birth of children is seen as a fulfillments of the commandment of procreation. A few anecdotes amplify this position. As a child, Joseph Soloveitchick was once reading the Psalms on the High Holidays as an expression of piety. His father approached him and replaced his son's Book of Psalms with a book of Jewish laws, saying "the service of God is identical with the study of Jewish law" (Soloveitchick, 1944, pg. 706) In another anecdote, a person in charge of blowing the ram's horn (shofar) once began to show tears before the performance of this commandment. He was approached and told to restrain his emotions while he was performing the divine will. Soloveitchick is a prime exponent of the behavioristic, rational and legalistic approach towards religion.

III. Religious Practice

The dual theoretical framework described above has shown itself at the practical level as well. Allport (1966) distinguished between an extrinsic and an intrinsic religious orientation. An extrinsic orientation means that religious devotion is not a value in its own right, but is an instrumental value serving the motives of persons, such as comfort, security, or social status (Allport, 1966, p. 6). Examples of this approach are reflected in: "What religion offers me most is comfort when sorrows and misfortune strike," and "one reason for my being a church member is that such membership helps to establish a person in the community" (Allport, 1966, p.6).

In contrast, intrinsic orientation, "regards faith as a supreme value in its own right" (Allport, 1966, p.6). Such faith strives to rise above personal needs. An example of this attitude is reflected in: "My religious beliefs are what really lie behind my whole approach to life" (Allport, 1966, p. 6).

Empirically, however, a third group and pattern also emerges. Allport refers to them as "inconsistently proreligious." They generally like religion and they accept both intrinsically and extrinsically worded statements, although these may be contradictory. For this group, religion has social desirability.

Allport's (1950, 1960) distinction between the types of religiousness is not merely the extent of a person's religious behavior, but suggests motives for his behavior, and to some extent the consequences in other aspects of his life.

Lenski (1963) also defined religious commitment in two ways. He distinguished between the socioreligious group which involves the commitment to a type of religious orientation which is highly individualistic and transcends group lines. The individualistic orientation stresses the solitariness of the religious actor. The collectivist orientation stresses the importance of collective corporate religious activity. Basically, Allport and Lenski have similar dichotomies but assign different terms to these religious orientations.

Glock (1962) delineated five dimensions of commitment or "religiosity" as different ways in which an individual can be religious. These include: (1) religious belief as the ideological dimension, which includes the specific doctrines about what people believe and think about religion; (2) religious practice as the ritual dimension, which includes participation and attendance at worship services, but takes into account the variations which exist in particular forms of religious practice; (3) religious feelings as the experiential dimension, which includes the subjective element of direct knowledge as a religious emotion of assurance; (4) religious knowledge as the intellectual dimension, which includes how much participants know about their religion; (5) and finally, religious effects as the consequential dimension, which includes the implications for practical conduct, reward, and responsibility. This is what the participant is expected to do and receive because of his religious commitment.

Glock concluded that research must focus on the interrelatedness of these dimensions. These areas are not independent but interdependent and must be measured together if the degree of commitment is to be determined. Glock did not suggest that highly committed participants would score high on a measure in every dimension. In fact, he cited Fukuyama's (1962) study developed a typology according to types of religious participation. The four major styles he identified are: (1) the intellectually oriented, participants who are well informed and view the sermon as something to think about; (2) the organizationally oriented, participants who are active and faithful in attendance and contribution to the church; (3) the belief oriented participants who consider beliefs important in defining their religious position; (4) the devotionally oriented, participants who emphasize feeling and emotion–the experiential part of religion.

The position of American psychology regarding religion has been a puzzling one. With the notable exceptions of William James (1902), Gordon Allport (1950), and a few others, most of psychology's key figures have ignored religious commitment and experience as worthy of investigation. Except for a small, peripheral group of people who have done research on the psychology of religion, most American psychologists have preferred to disregard religion or to adopt an antagonistic position such as was heralded by Freud (1913).

IV. Man's Search for His Soul

The integration of practice and knowledge with belief and experience is the road to spirituality. This unity is experienced as a fusion with God and an obliteration of the self.

Throughout the history of Judaism various movements have arisen, both from within and outside of it, that have emphasized the road to spirituality by bifurcating body and soul, manifestation and essence, flesh and spirit, humanity and divinity, and extrinsic and intrinsic religious orientation.

From within Judaism, the Essenes strove for spirituality while emphasizing a life of asceticism. The Reform movement which arose in the 19th century accentuated the prophetic vision of social justice without the normative structure of *Halakhah*.

Coming out of Judaism, Christianity arose from a striving to achieve spirituality without the "form" of *Halakhah* as well.

Similarly, within Orthodoxy two groups formed in the 18th century which embraced different emphases. The *Chasidic* movement stressed the simple man's way of reaching God through feeling, even if it is devoid of knowledge, which is the way chosen by the *Mitnagdim*. The former is exemplified by the following anecdote.

OPENING THE GATES OF REPENTANCE

A young illiterate herdsman who lived alone during the year came on the Day of Atonement to the synagogue of the Baal Shem Tov. Although the lad was unable to join the congregation in prayer, he grasped the significance and spirit of the occasion as the day wore on. He experienced a strong, overwhelming emotion to participate with the congregation in pleading for atonement. As the Neilah service was drawing to a close, the herdsman took from his pocket a reed whistle he used while tending his flock and blew on it lustily.

Hearing the solemn sanctity of the Neilah thus disturbed, the Chasidim angrily upbraided the lad. However, the Baal Shem Tov, in a calm, decisive voice took his followers to task:

"Despite all your prayers, your learning and piety, you have not learned to repent, nor have you been able to prevail upon God to grant you pardon. This illiterate young herdsman, possessed with a sincere desire to serve the Almighty, has opened the gates of repentance for all of us."

The Chasidic movement also emphasizes the enjoyment of life in the performance of *Halakhah*. Nevertheless certain of their sects are antinomian, particularly in reference to observance of specific time in the performance of morning, afternoon and evening prayers.

The movement that *Chasidus* arose against, the *Mitnagdim*, scrupulously observe every detail of *Halakhah*. Through this observance of minutiae, people feel that they are fulfilling the will of God. Anecdotes reflecting this movement have been mentioned previously in connection with Rabbi Joseph Soloveitchick. The *Mitnagdim* ascribe 'objective' meaning to their observance but unfortunately do not necessarily imbue their behavior with subjective piety, spirituality, or emotion.

V. The Unity of Humanity and Divinity

The experience of striving for the numinous requires a special preparation of time and centering. It can take place both with a group, in a dyad or by oneself. But it always takes place as a fusion of man and God. This fusion is transitory and usually eludes the modern Jewish person. Why? In order to achieve this union one has to be aware of one's psyche. "Psyche" is a Greek word connoting man's soul or spirit.

Modern man is frequently insufficiently aware of himself. He is easily distracted and frequently deceives himself regarding the truth of himself or relationship. Modern man has much difficulty in centering and focusing.

The Torah provides very few examples of the numinous experience. Not only are there few of these, their absence is particularly noteworthy. Not one numinous expression in the Akeda (Abraham's sacrifice of Isaac) story!

A few numinous experiences which are mentioned in the Torah are noteworthy.

In Exodus 3:6 after an angel of God appears to him via a burning bush, Moses conceals his face because he is afraid to look at God. This experience is so overwhelming that his first reaction is to recoil from the reality of it. Moses reacts to God's presence by attempting to diminish the experience.

In Genesis 17:3 prior to Avram's metamorphosis to Abraham, He falls on his face when he hears that his children will continue the covenant that was between God and himself. Interestingly, God continues his discourse with him as if He were unaware of Abraham's religious experience and trepidation.

In Deuteronomy 5:22-25, the people ask never again to hear God's voice because the experience of the theophany is too overwhelming. Since the people are afraid that they will die under similar circumstances, God chooses to speak to the people via a prophet.

Perhaps Rudolph Otto's thesis in the *Idea of the Holy* is really demonstrated in the Bible: the numinous is ineffable and any attempt at describing it not only falls short but actually does it injustice.

VI. Why is Man Destined to Die?

The thesis of this paper is that the creation of man is an attempt to unify man and God, spirit and flesh. This creation of dramatically opposed entities can only co-exist for a finite time period. Man is given the opportunity to strive to unity, to struggle against overwhelming difficult odds to achieve a balance whereby flesh is in the service of spirit and spirit is in the service of flesh.

Recognizing the insurmountable challenge which God has given man, God states in Genesis 6:3, "My *Spirit* shall not be in man forever since his is also composed of *flesh* therefore his days shall be 120 years." God recognizes the ultimate futility of eternal coexistence of diametrically opposite forces.

VII. The Ultimate Challenge

Gabriel Marcel (1950), a French existentialist, stated that "Life is not a problem to be solved but a challenge to be lived." Rabbi Joseph Solveitchick (1944) stated that "Against my will I was born and against my will I will die, but through my will I will live." These two terse but very poignant statements reflect my philosophy as well. Man, by recognizing the difficulty in his existence, has achieved a heightened awareness of God, himself and life. Through this new realization, man continues the ultimate struggle of searching for permanent unity of body and soul in a transient time of 120 years.

REFERENCES

1. Allport, G.W. *The Individual and His Religion: A Psychological Interpretation.* New York: MacMillan, 1950.
2. Allport, G.W. *Religion in the Developing Personality.* New York: University Press, 1960.
3. Allport, G.W. "Traits Revisited." *American Psychologist,* 1966, 21, 1-10
4. Freud S. *Totem and Taboo.* London: Routledge and Kegan Paul, 1950. Original published 1913.
5. Fukuyama, Y. "The Major Dimensions of Church Membership." *Review of Religious Research,* 1961, 2, 154-161.
6. Glock, C.Y. "On the Study of Religious Commitment." *Religious Edition, Research Supplement,* 1962, 57, S98-S110.
7. Heller, Aryeh Leib. *Kezot ha-Hoshen.* Jerusalem: Pardes, 5720.
8. James W. *The Varieties of Religious Experience,* Garden City, New York: Dolphin Books, 1902.
9. Leeuw, G. van der. *Religion in Essence and Manifestation.* New York: Harper, 1963. Originally published, 1933.

10. Lenski, G. *The Religious Factor*. New York: Doubleday and Co., Inc., 1963.

11. Marcel G. *The Mystery of Being*. Regenery, Chicago, 1950.

12. Soloveitchick, J.B. "Man of Halakhah." (Hebrew) *Talpioth* 1944, 1, 651-735, Reprinted *Halakhic Man*, translated by Lawrence Kaplan, The Jewish Publication Society of America, 1983.

13. Twersky, I. "Religion and Law." *Religion in a Religious Age*, S.D. Goiten (Ed.). Cambridge, Massachusetts: Ktav Publishing House, 1974.

A Jewish Mystical Movement
Yisroel Ben Baruch Ha Chassid

In the view of the majority of Occidental students of mysticism there obtain two main divisions of occult philosophy: the Yoga of the East whose principal authority is Patanjali; and the Qabalah of the West.

There exists, however, yet another and most significant system of Jewish Mysticism–*Chassidism*–concerning which surprisingly little appears to be known. In the works of W. Wynn Westcott and Arthur Edward Waite there are casual statements as to the existence of the Chassidism–and no more. This revivalist movement is, in reality, so important and of so recent a date, that I am moved to present a few of its major tenets. Those which have most strongly impressed me are given here, hand in hand with some verbatim statements of those of its exponents who rightfully acquired the laudatory title of *Tsaddik* or saint, together with a few comparatively and explanatory remarks on the Qabalah.

As early as the eighth century A.D. the *Sepher Yetsirah* made its first appearance publicly. Tradition subscribes to the theory that the *Sepher haZohar*, the main textbook of doctrinal Qabalah, appearing during the thirteenth century, was written in the first instance by Rabbi Simeon ben Yochai in the third century. To its ideology a great deal of attention was attracted from both Jewish and Christian scholars. Bitter controversy ensued on questions of religious doctinralia and origins, with the result that gradually it became known in almost every Jewish community throughout Europe.

The appearance, therefore, of the Chassidischer Movement among the Polish and Ukrainian Jews in the first half of the eighteenth century need occasion no astonishment or surprise as to the source of its inspiration. The book constituting that mass of religious literature which, in its entirety, is comprehended as the Qabalah has penetrated into every nook and cranny of Europe. Spain had become one of the earliest centres of the Qabalistic schools, whose missionaries spread the secret doctrine wherever they went. From Palestine it flowed into Italy. From Italy it penetrated Central Europe. It then proceeded to Germany, Poland and Russia. All of these countries possessed large Jewish communities, a few of whose Rabbis had become enthused by the rousing ecstasies of the *Zohar* of ben Yochai and the Lurian methods of spiritual development. In the meanwhile, vicious polemical attacks had been published by the orthodox Rabbinical authorities against the widely spreading mysticism of the Qabalah, and in consequence the ordinary mass of Jews had not adequate means of ascertaining what constituted its true nature. No serious attempt had been made to popularize its teachings. The greater proportion of its exponents were overzealous and egotistical, inflamed with spiritual pride and self-conceit.

By the end of the seventeenth century the Jewish religion had become crystalized into a set of forms from which every vestige of vitality had fled. In the Talmud the early Rabbis had codified a considerable number of ceremonies, regulations and observances which came to be regarded *in toto* as the Jewish religion. There were, for instance, a highly complex procedure for purifying the house on Passover, rituals for the correct slaughter of animals, ceremonials pertaining to the order of services in the home, methods of afflicting the soul during the High Holy Days, and rules as to *how* and *when* and what prayers should be said. In consequence the noblest ideals of spirituality among the Jews were no loftier than the eating of *Matzohs* on Passover, *Chumentash* on Purim, the lighting of eight candles during *Chanukah*, and the fasting on *Yom Kippur*. Yet this hard and fast creed, divorced from all spirituality, continued obstinately perpetrated by progroms and persecution erected a gigantic constricting barricade around this Talmudic edifice, beyond which the Jews, in peril of race-annihilation, feared to wander.

In the twelfth century Rabbi Moseh ben Maimon, affected by the hair-splitting Scholastic philosophy, endeavored to rationalize Judaism. He insisted that all dogmas should dogmas should coincide with the Aristotelian philosophy, and that no other interpretation should be admitted other than that which accorded with purely intellectual principles.

Judaism was virtually dying, despite the presence of the Qabalah and a few fanatical Qabalistic philosophers. The latter had incurred disrepute by reason of their fanaticism, self-righteousness, and superstitions, following upon their refusal or inability to apply systematic scepticism to their beliefs and visions. They missed the great opportunity of revitalizing the exoteric religion with an esoteric philosophy and a practical mystical system.

And then, out of the blackness, came a spark which subsequently ignited the whole of the people of Israel.

About 1700 there was born in Poland–in Okop, I believe–one who was destined to become known as *Baal Shem Tov*. His real name was Israel ben Eliezer. As a boy, Israel was appointed beadle to the local synagogue, there receiving the opportunity of learning Torah and Talmud, wherein, while proficient, there was no display of Hebrew dialectic or genius. He was, essentially, a mystic, and the dry husks of the Torah left his eager soul hungry and unappeased. Later, legend has it, when he literally ached and thirsted after God, but did not find Him in Rabbinism, he departed from the village, and in wandering amongst the primordial forests of the Carpathians he opened himself to the Spirit of Inspiration. He yearned for divine intimacy with a passion which in its sheer simplicity and grandeur is at once touching and inspiring, commanding respect and reverence from all. This seeking after solitude, wherein to commune with the Soul of Nature, became the example of subsequent *Tsaddikim*, and inspired one of the most eminent Chassids of a later day, Rabbi Nachman of Bratslaw, to enjoin his disciples:

Solitude is the highest state. Only in solitude can man attain to the abnegation of the Ego *(bitul hoyesh)* **and thus attain union with the eternal God.**

Listening eagerly to the singing of birds, the youthful Baal Shem came to understand and love their songs. He learned of life from the secret whispering of the leaves touched by gentle breezes, from the hum of the bee in quest of honey, and from the quiet, sensitive steps of the deer. In all the manifestations of Nature he saw the terror and splendour of God, too. The terrific thunderstorm of mid-Continent, the vivid lightning, the rushing of the river, the cheery burbling of the stream as through meadow and vale it wound its way, and the awe of the snow-clad peaks of the mountains–all these contributed an indelible impression which was seared into his very soul. So unquenchable was his devotion, and so tremendous was the depth of his yearning, that according to legend,

Sometimes he walked in his deep meditations three days and three nights and no food of any kind passed his lips.

And there in solitude and in the silence, under the open sky, with God on all sides surrounding him, he found himself. In the quiet of his own inner consciousness, in the dark fastness of the heart of the forests, and amid the grim secret womb of the grey mountains, the secret of Nature was yielded to him. The solution to the problems of God, Man, and the World was made known to his enquiring spirit. Into his quiescent *Ruach* whose whirlpool modifications and turbulence had been stilled by an iron will and by the force of his constant prayer, there was poured, as into a receptive Chalice of pure gold, an awe-inspiring vision–a staggering revelation of infinite dimension. It burst upon him violently in a single moment. He *knew* by an intuition in which there was no element of self-doubt, *why* he had come to this earth, and *what* the destiny required of him.

Back to the throes of civilization he retraced his footsteps and, gathering to his sacred banner a number of sincere individuals, he quietly taught them Enlightenment and the True Way of Life. Then, following an ancient example, he sent missionaries and apostles all over the country-side of Poland, to Ukraine, Russia, Lithuania, and Galicia, arousing the inert populace to greater religious fervour and devotion with the preaching of human and divine love and the doctrine of the inflaming of the soul to ecstasy. Some of his zealous young Rabbis, so intent upon spreading the new gospel, wandered as far afield as Palestine–the mystical seat of the *Shechinah*. To these mystics the desolate Canaan of their day and the Land of Promise of the past were one and the same.

Such was the reputation of Rabbi Israel ben Eliezer for piety and sanctity, and such the spiritual force and splendour which radiated from his noble personality, that he soon earned from his co-religionists unbounded respect and reverence, and the complimentary title of The Master of The Good Name. Vast numbers of people have testified to his "Christlike" character. Not only was he "Christlike" in this respect and that of the vividness of his illumination, but tradition tells that he walked amongst the people in the villages, healing the sick in body and soul. He comforted the bereaved; hc cast out demons with his magical exorcisms, and prognosticated the future. Is it any wonder that the people flocked to him?

Little of actuality is known of this spiritual giant. What has come down to us is so covered over by accretions of superstition that it is difficult to obtain a clear picture of the grandeur and majesty of the personality of him who came to be known familiarly as

Besht. His teaching, however, persists. Even today there are Chassidim, although their mysticism exists in a regrettably degenerate form. With care, we are able to sift from a dry heap of doctrinal chaff the heart and kernel of what Baal Shem did preach to the Jews of his time.

In this dispensation of Baal Shem Tov *Hislahabus* was the prime doctrine. *Hislahabus* is the pivotal centre of Chassidism. Baal Shem taught, first of all, the "aim of man is to be the Temple of God," and that the "essence and aim of the *Torah* is love to God and devotion to Him." Love of God and man, under every circumstance, was the alpha and omega of the teaching. *Hislahabus* therefore is ecstasy, the spiritual fire kindled in the innermost core of one who devotes himself wholly to God. It is an all-consuming combustion of the soul, self-awakened; the ardour of ecstasy, in whose indivisible light all that was and will be appears simple and united. Chassidism and *Hislahabus* were the revolt of devotion and love and fervent religion against the sterility of intellectual legalism and sham. The Chassidim learnt to worship God with a fiery enthusiasm which seemed to break all the bonds of the traditional ceremonial, thus incurring the enmity of orthodoxy and vested authority. Dancing and Joy and Song came to be the keynotes of their worship. One, Rabbi Nachman, to whom reference has already been made, expressed himself on this subject as follows:

> **All creation resolves itself into melody…Faith in God has its own melody, the most important in the world, affecting all others…Heaven and earth are saturated with song. The man who hears this melody becomes purified and inspired to lead a new life, especially if he can understand also the dance, which produces a complete harmony through its rhythm. Every limb of the body contains in itself a rhythm in the whole body, of the feet an so forth…The melody appears more complete if it is fitted with words, because the rhythms of verses in combination with the melody produces a harmony. How splendid it is to hear this and to see it supplemented by dancing!**

And among the Tsaddikim, legend is current that there were very few like this Rabbi Nachman, so enthusiastic about song and dancing. In this respect the Chassidischer movement would remind one of Sri Chaitanya of the fifteenth century. Certainly it recalls to mind the blessed Sri Ramakrishna Paramahamsa, whose frequent Sankirtans and singing of sacred song were so passionate and fervent, fraught with divine emotion, that changes of a far reaching character–moral, intellectual and spiritual–were wrought in the hearts of disciples and devotees who observed his ecstatic dancing and clapping of hands.

Baal Shem taught of *Kavanah*, the redemption of all Nature through action, and the self-dedication to sanctity. *Kavanah* is a hallowed song of the glory of God, the *Schechinah*, dwelling in all men. It is redemption and regeneration, and it as said that this is the meaning and purpose of *Kavanah*, that it is given to mankind in order that they may lift up those who are fallen and set free the sparks of light and life imprisoned in the forms about us. *Kavanah* leads to *Hislahabus* which, Professor Martin Buber writes, "is the cup of grace, the key to the eternal." This ecstasy of *Hislahabus* is the way and the end of the individual; it is likened to a "rope stretched over the Abyss"–the Abyss between God and man. Nietzsche's famous statement that man was but a bridge over an abyss–a connecting link between lower forms of existence and the Superman foreshadowed by Zarathustra–finds a precedent here. For verily *Hislahabus* bequeaths to an individual just those rare divine qualities which raise him beyond his fellows. The genuine *Tsaddik* or saint gives one a fleeting vision whither the onrushing stream of evolution carries us. The Zoharists previously had spoken of the Divine Kiss, when the *Neschamah* comes face to face with the Beloved, its Creator, and the vision of Beatitude and Beauty is so ravishing, so rich, so divinely sweet and intoxicant, that straightaway it swoons into ecstasy and unites with the Root of all. So also is *Hislahabus*.

It is ever silent. Ecstasy is speechless with the exuberant fullness of emotion, always without words or concrete expression; for it lies in bliss in the warm and boundless heart of the most high.

The foundation of all Chassidic teaching, perpetually reiterated in every preaching, was the immanence of God. "Everything," said Baal Shem, "is created and formed from God's being, as the tortoise and its covering are completely one." There was one Tsaddik, Rabbi Schneur Salomon, who, just two days before the Angel of Death overtook him, said, "I can only see the Spirit of everything." This feeling of conscious worship pervades the entirety of Chassid literature, demonstrating the real illumination which had come to them.

In the Qabalah, from which Chassidism developed, and which, in consequence, coloured the entire thought of the Tsaddikim, God is conceived of as *Ain Soph*, the Infinite, from which the whole universe with multitudinous variety of forms and natural kingdoms, has evolved. It is the One Life, sustaining and vivifying all things. A pre-Zoharic Qabalist, Rabbi Azariel ben Menachem, has written that by the *Ain Soph* he understood "A Being Infinite, boundless, identical with itself, united with itself, without attributes, will, intention, desire, thought, word or deed." This is a philosophical conception which is at once identical with the Parabrahman of the Vedanta and the Absolute of European idealists. If the Absolute is without attributes of any kind, then the human mind is unable to comprehend it as it really is in and for itself. In a certain sense, it is, therefore Nothing. The Qabalist definitely implied this when stating that God is *Ain*. Naught, and between this ontological formulation and that of the Non-Being of Hegel a distinct parallelism is established.

The same metaphysical conception was retained by the Chassidim, although in a more or less anthropomorphized form; and to it was ascribed an inscrutable and sublimated personality to suit the needed and requirements of the simple unintelligent folk to whom the Mysticism was taught. It would seem evident that the people require something more definite and tangible than an ontological abstraction. That is abstraction of pure philosophy had supreme Reality the *Tsaddikim* had no doubt. It was, at the beginning, an effort to elevate the religious-minded masses by a warmer–though perhaps cruder definition of Deity. But the true spiritual idea was never wholly forsaken, regardless of how much it would appear to be so from an exoteric point of view. Here and there we find teachings demonstrating that the original doctrine was well-remembered and cherished as a sacred trust. As an instance, one Chassidic Master said:

> **The Creation of heaven and earth is the unfolding of something out of Nothing, the descent of the higher into the lower. But the saints…turn that which is something back into that which is Nothing. And still, more wonderful, they lift up above that which is below.**

Indubitably this remark reveals that the greatest teachers of this religious movement never wavered from the truth nor completely lost sight of the initiated philosophy. Though God and union with God must ever be the perspective to be kept before the Vision of the soul, the degradation of the concept of God ensues if to Him are ascribed attributes and qualities of too human a character.

They propounded at length the teaching that God indwelt the Universe, that he had made it, and that he abided its Separate Lord. Each form, each molecule of that form, every constituent atom of that minute speck, was pervaded by that one Sacred Life-Spirit, Consciousness, God, call it what you will. I quote Professor Buber once again:

> **The distinctive idea of the Chassids seems to be that of the immanence of God. They picture Him at first, before the Creation, alone, complete, supreme. Then from the void He created the Universe and in so doing sent forth from Himself His own glory or presence–the Shekinah–(which found a fit habitation) not only in man himself, and in all his thoughts and qualities, but also in animals, in vegetables, and even in inanimate things.**

Within each microscopic speck of dust there dwelt a Spark of divinity. A Soul had enthroned itself therein. And the *Tsaddik* who attained to *Kavanah* could aid all the sparks in Nature to the ultimate redemption of all. Thus the Jewish economy reveals itself in Mystical Philosophy. Nothing is to be wasted. There is no refuse to be thrown as on to a dust-heap of the universe. But the whole Cosmos is spirit and matter in evolution together.

The identical dictum is postulated in the Qabalah. From *Ain Soph* there evolve Sephiros or spiritual potencies wherein resides the innate impulse to grow and progress. The highest of these *Sephiros* is *Keser*, the Crown, which is the One Spiritual Monad, formulated in the infinitudes of Space as a metaphysical centre of spiritual force, a minute point of consciousness which is everywhere. From *Keser* are emanated other *Sephiros*, culminating eventually in the Sephirah *Malkus*, the Kingdom, which is that physical world tangible to our normal sense, cognition, and perception. "Kesser is in Malkus, and Malkus is in Keser–but after another manner," says the Zohar. There are ten Sephiros, but in them, of them, and around them is the Presence of the Ancient of Ancients, Blessed be He.

These *Tsaddikim* indeed were God-intoxicated philosophers. Certainly "God-intoxicated" seems more relevant and applicable to these pious Chassidim than to a formal academic like Spinoza. For in the hearts of these men of piety there flamed a fire of love, love inexhaustible and forever reaching out to their fellow man. Verily their overflowing stream of love was like the magnet, drawing all things near to it, and imparting to them that same vital warmth of fervent devotion. Whatever they did, were it eating, drinking, sleeping, God was present in their minds and souls, and all was done to the glory and honour of God.

Reincarnation is another doctrine which finds place in both the Zoharic and Chassidic doctrines. Rabbi Chayim Vital was the author, in the seventeenth century of a work entitled *Gilgolem*, where was expounded the prevailing Qabalistic ideas of reincarnation. There is an old Chassidic legend of a Rabbi whose house was famed far and wide, for it possessed a leather-bound, time-scarred, hand-worn volume–a work of Rabbi Yitzhok Luria. This shows, more or less, to what extent the Qabalah was venerated. Such being the case, one would logically anticipate Reincarnation to be one of the articles of belief in the developed teaching of Baal Shem Tov. So true is this that numerous legends persist of *Tsaddikim*, wonderful saints and adepts learned in the mysteries of existence and wise in Chassidic lore, who could remember with incredible ease their past lives and their earlier forms of growth. Their previous incarnations were as familiar to them as memory of a preceding week or month is to us. They were certain of their own future as of their own heartbeats. The disciples of Rabbi Nachman knew that their Master remained with them forever. Previous to death he had lived amongst them, and they said with naivete, now that he is dead, he has chosen the grave for the abode of his body. It was, in their eyes, as though he had simply passed from one room in a house to another, and if they called to him he would surely hear.

That Baal Shem, the first of the great Chassidim, was a mystic, and a very fine one, is amply corroborated by the stories of those who were privileged to know him. From his wan face a lustre of spiritual radiance was emitted; and his large deep eyes–fraught with wisdom of higher spheres–shone with a glory that was not man's His personality was so pure and gracious that thousands flocked merely to see him and to hear him speak. His surpassing stature coincides perfectly, in my estimation, with the great Mahatmas who figure in the legends of the East and of all ages and of all climes. In accordance with the traditions of old time, he gathered pupils unto himself, and bestowed upon the most worthy of them the esoteric training that is as old as the world itself. His direct successor, Rabbi Baer ben Abraham, gives us a glimpse into the nature of that training when he writes that Baal Shem Tov:

> ...taught me the language of the birds and of the trees. He revealed to me the secrets of the saints and the magic spells. He led me into the book "Meine haChochmah" and explained every letter to me...In the book "Ratziel" he showed me the writing of the angels, and explained to me that certain letters of the alphabet corresponded to the angels, according to the significance of each angel and of his origin, in this or in the next world.

As proof authentic that Chassidism, at its inception, was a genuine and profound mystical movement, inspired by a genius of overwhelming capabilities, teaching the honourable doctrines of the Age-old Wisdom inherent in the Soul itself, Baal Shem Tov taught adeptship as the purposed of evolution and the goal of all aspiration. He put before the populace the ideal of the attainment of a supernal state of consciousness, wherein man ceases to be and becomes God-Man. In the adept, was his doctrine, is all life realized. In the one in whom Spirit and Matter have become equilibrized, and in whose *Ruach* the light of ever-living *Yechidah* shines with undimmed radiance and immortality, in him has Nature perfected itself, and consummated the fruition of the ages. In the acquisition of Hislahabus, and in the solemn repetition of its sublime ecstasies, is the finality of thraldom, the sloughing off of the very chains of bondage and illusion. He has, as the Hindus would say, attained Moksham. And the man who is permanently aflame with ardour has command over life and control over death, and no outward even that intrudes within the hallowed sphere of his saintly activities can disturb his sanctity. Both in the philosophy of the Qabalah and Baal Shem, the enlightened man is above everything else in the universe, beyond even the angels and the gods. The adept is the Elect of the World. For, as Professor Buber says:

> The Angels rest in God, but he saints move forward. The Angel is stationary, and the saint is a traveller. Therefore is the saint above the Angel...Above nature and above time and above thought, thus is he named who lives in Hislahabus... He makes of his body a throne of life, and of life a throne of the spirit, and of the spirit a throne of the light of the Glory of God, and the light streams round about him, and he sits in the midst of the light and trembles and rejoices.

After the death of Baal Shem Tov at the age of 60 years there several exceedingly pious *Tsaddiks*, and, in fact, legend has it that one of them, the venerable Rabbi Nachman of Bratzlaw, was as great a *Tsaddik*, perhaps greater, than the Master. Born in 1772 in Miedzeboz he showed great promise as a child, and from early boyhood on he studied the Qabalah of Rabbi Yitzhok Luria. At one time, finding that some distance from the village there was a high mountain, at the summit of which was a large crevice or cave, Rabbi Nachman, impressed with the technique of Luria's asceticism, left the village, and in this cave was fond of sitting quietly thinking about God. Sometimes he would walk, in a spirit of awe and admiration, through the forests, which bestowed upon him a portion of their strength and fulfillment. In the summer he would row a boat on a river, and on its silent bosom become absorbed in meditation and prayer. In him too, did *Hislahabus* make hast to arise, and thereafter his ecstasies were almost a common occurrence.

He taught that the secret of discovering God was inflaming oneself with prayer–just as Abramelin the Mage, centuries previously, had done in teaching of the attainment of the Knowledge and Conversation of the Holy Guardian Angel. Man, Rabbi Nachman said, must lose himself in prayer and entirely forget his own identity and existence. "It is as if one stood before a king," he narrates in parable to his disciples, "and surrendered all thought of oneself in order to concentrate entirely on the king." "A man must gather each letter, each syllable to form them into words, the words of prayer." And from the very depths thereof, so that one's mind becomes single-minded, concentrated. Then, when the mind is one-pointed, and the Soul willfully inflamed to fever pitch, there takes place that experience which is the Flower of Life. In the doctrine of Samadhi, Hindu doctrine is comparable. In every mysticism, in every scheme of occult philosophy, the same ideas are expressed.

Those who followed the dictates of Baal Shem and his immediate successors attained to a similar spiritual communion, and thus kept the chain unbroken. Those young missionaries, inspired by Baal Shem Tov and Rabbi Baer and Rabbi Nachman of Bratzlaw, wandered about for the rest of their lives, praying, teaching, and exemplifying in daily practice the philosophy to which they subscribed. They were saints of great spiritual strength and nobility of purpose. Salomon Maimon (b. 1754 in Lithuania) narrates the story of a young Chassid missionary whose personal acquaintance he made. This *Tsaddik* was a young man, hardly more than twenty-two years of age, not very strong physically, rather pale in complexion, and somewhat thin in build. Yet in his appearance there was something terrible and majestic. Something which demanded obedience, and which curtailed all argument. It enable him to rule the people in his village with a despotic sway. And in his stern eyes there was a glint which inspired imperious ardour in the hearts of all who heard his preaching. A great Talmudic scholar of that day who refused to accept the doctrines of Baal Shem, and ridiculed the ideas of *Hislahabus* and spiritual ecstasy, was so terrified by a look which he received from his young *Tsaddik* that he was taken away in a high fever. Very soon after that incident he went to the grave.

Here my account of the Chassidim must end. There is so much to write on this subject, and I have been able to give only the briefest and most fragmentary of accounts. Just as Samadhi in the central attainment of the true Yoga, so *Hislahabus* is to Chassidism. The Chassidic legends cannot dwell long enough on examples of divine favour which shines upon the single-minded ardent man, nor of the potency of his services. And just as Ishvara leading ultimately to Parabrahman was the goal set up by the Yoga, so God as *Ain Soph* was the ultimate of the *Tsaddik*.

Unfortunately, like every other mystical or religious movement, with the death of the greater Founder and his immediate successors who carried in their hearts the inspiration and message of the Master, this Movement gradually lost its vigour and strength and spirituality. Having spread originally among an almost entirely illiterate and uneducated people, superstitions–intended primarily to magnify, laud, and aggrandize the character of the Man they loved and venerated–soon became rife and popular. And today, it has completely degenerated. It still persists in a mild form.

Whether this Movement will ever be revived again is difficult to say. Its resuscitation is an urgent necessity. The present status of Judaism is very much like unto what it was in the days of the Master–even worse. For the modern spirit of Jewry breathes forth disruption and dispersion, and the spirit of the Chassidim is required to bind them together once again into an unbreakable whole. It is to be hoped that the inspiration of the Chassidim and the power of the Tsaddikim will descend from above and animate a religious genius of our time to point out, not only to the Jews but to all mankind, the noble path which leads to Reality, without which, and without the ecstasy of *Hislahabus* the whole of their lives, and the sum total of their strivings and wanderings, are as naught.

Part Two

THOUGHT AND JUDAISM:
The Wisdom of the Psyche

*"Spirit, like God, denotes an object of
psychic experience which cannot be proved
to exist in the external world and cannot
be understood rationally."*
–C.G. Jung

Illustration by Martin Mondrus

In Search of One's Missing Soul
Daryl Dovid Temkin

A phenomenon impacting the American Jewish community for the past two decades has been the "return" of a significant number of its young adults to traditional Jewish values and life styles. The last three generations of Jews have witnessed a movement from close observance of Jewish tradition to wide-spread secularization and non-observance. Within this current period of secularization, there has developed a group of Jews who, through a search for their own identity–their missing soul–have returned to the observance of traditional Jewish practices.

This process of "return" has typically taken place among Jews who were raised in assimilated, secular, Reform, or Conservative Jewish homes. The religious background of these homes commonly had grandparents or at least great-grandparents who were steeped in traditional Jewish life. For a number of reasons, the proceeding generations either liberalized their religious practices or totally rejected traditionally Judaism.

Many immigrant Jews felt that after leaving the "old country" of Europe or Russia, it was no longer proper or necessary to retain active Jewish identifications. It became of utmost importance for the new immigrants to blend into the "melting pot," to be accepted as Americans and not to stand out as Jews. These Jews thought that by upholding the Jewish tradition, they would be separating themselves from the American society. If they would retain their separate ways, it was feared that this type of behavior might open doors for a new wave of anti-Semitism from which so many of them had recently escaped.

Others left Judaism because they thought that it was archaic and therefore no longer relevant to the modern scientific age. Those who felt ideologically estranged from traditional Judaism chose alternative ways of relating to religious values. Some chose to identify with one of the non-Orthodox branches of Judaism, others opted for humanistic secularism, and there were those who chose conversion to a more socially acceptable religion, namely Christianity. The majority of Jews remained in some type of Jewish affiliation and built a modern, secularized Jewish home.

In the modern, secularized Jewish home, the extent of Jewish education provided for the children ranged from being non-existent to limited bar/bat mitzvah–confirmation training. For most Jewish children, the bar/bat mitzvah training was an educational farce. This traditionally significant passage of life ceremony tended to be divested of almost all of its religious and spiritual qualities.

For many Jewish families, the bar/bat mitzvah event was a gift collecting affair where the parents showed off their party giving skills and the child retained the memory of how much money he or she collected. Instead of signifying the religiously intended beginning of Jewish commitment and Jewish educational growth, the bar/bat mitzvah ceremony typically marked the end of the child's Jewish education.

Furthermore, the non-traditional Jewish home placed a great significance on the importance of pursuing a quality secular education and attaining a respectable profession. It minimized the significance of a Jewish education. These homes rarely placed importance on participating in Jewish communal activities. They tended to neglect the observance of Jewish holidays. In many instances, these homes lost all awareness that Shabbat or Jewish holidays even existed. It became customary for the family members to go out to a football game, a movie, or a party on a Friday night rather than the family being home together to sanctify the Shabbat.

Interestingly enough, no matter how much "Jewish erosion" had taken place in a family, there was one central Jewish value which parent expected their children to know and to fully observe. This was the expectation for the child not to marry outside of the Jewish faith. Although interdating may have been permitted if not encouraged for the child's overall growth, intermarriage remained a clear and unquestionable taboo.

In spite of the taboo, the effects of interdating along with the secularization of the Jewish family led to many cases of intermarriage. The *Jewish Yearbook 1971* stated that 45% of Jews were intermarrying. Jewish parents faced with their children coming home with a non-Jewish mate selection, were found speechless. How could these parents suddenly begin to teach their children Jewish values and background when the family has chosen long ago to basically neglect these issues?

The college and post college years are a time when young Jews begin to seriously confront, question, and search for their personal identity. Philosophical as well as practical questions concerning difficult topics as personal direction, values, ethics, identity, as well as what is the meaning and the purpose of life becomes most significant and perplexing. Students at this stage in life are often lonely, insecure, and vulnerable to various influences offering them directions and answers. Missionizing religions and cults enjoy taking full advantage of gathering recruits from this confused and needy population.

Jews who were seeking spiritual guidance and meaning had a tendency not to look towards Judaism. Their bar/bat mitzvah and inconsistent Jewish home experience left them with the concept that Judaism is at best shallow if not empty to meaningful practices and beliefs. In the last decades, many young Jews, challenged by the need to search for their identity, joined Eastern religions, ventured to India to study with a guru, converted to Christianity, became a Jew for Jesus, dropped out with drugs, or became recruited into a cult.

The majority of young Jews avoided the demands of this period of spiritual quest. Perhaps they circumvented these concerns by staying focused within their own career goals, by not having philosophical quests, by remaining in adherence to the values of secular society, or by already being grounded in the Jewish tradition. In contrast to the above mentioned situations, there were other Jews who, while in search for their identity, their missing soul, eventually found their way back to their own spiritual roots.

Following the victorious Israeli war of 1967, it became popular for college age Jews to venture to Israel. These students went to Israel in order to attend university, to work on a kibbutz, to tour, or to visit relatives. While in Israel, the opportunity arose for a number of these students not only to learn about their heritage but also to experience living it.

In post Nazi holocaust ear, 1967 marked the opening of the new age where it became acceptable for young people to be Jewish and to be proud of it. During this time, a number of schools offering intensive courses in Jewish religion were built in Israel. These schools were aimed at serving the needs of this American college age community who had grown up well-versed in secular knowledge but lacked the most elementary and fundamental knowledge of their own traditional religious identity.

These various institutions for Jewish learning, called "yeshivot," ("yeshiva" singular) were patterned after the age-old traditional Jewish schools in Europe. The typical curricula of this type of yeshiva offered new students an introduction to Judaism. They included studies in Jewish and contemporary issues and the study of traditional Jewish textual sources; Torah, Talmud, Codes of Jewish Law, mystical, philosophical and classical Jewish ethical texts.

The studies in the yeshivot allowed these Jews to learn the meaning and purpose behind their religious system. Through the yeshiva studies, light from Jewish tradition and Talmudic lore was shed on twentieth century questions in bio-ethics, sociology, business, psychology, and philosophy.

After completing the introductory yeshiva studies, Judaism was no longer viewed as mainly being a "lox and bagels" Sunday morning Jewish "soul food" brunch. These students discovered that Judaism had a much deeper, enlightening, and inspiring way of nourishing the soul.

The professors at Berkeley and Yale were no longer the exclusive models for ideals and success with these people. Goals, virtues, and values for conducting one's life, as well as for building a family and a society, were modeled to the students by the yeshiva's rabbis, their wives, and their families.

After a period of study, these students begin to put their learning into practice. Eventually, the full observance of the Shabbat, all the Jewish holidays, as well as the dietary laws of 'kashrut" became integrated into the lives of the modern-say yeshiva students. The study of Jewish ethics for daily living presented enlightening and enriching ways of seeing the world and living in it. Jewish ethics became intriguing areas for discussion as did the meaningfulness of religious practices.

These Jews added new dimensions to their being by incorporating a concept of God along with Judaism's system of "mitzvot," religious obligations. By fulfilling mitzvot, initial action was being taken towards completing one's responsibilities aimed at building a finer society. Thought the yeshiva experience, negative or ambivalent notions of Judaism were transformed into feeling of excitement, warmth and endless depth.

In contrast to their parents and grandparents, who had discarded or revised their participation in Judaism, these young, secularly educated Jews, trained as scientists, physicians, social workers, musicians, mathematicians, computer programmers, lawyers and businessmen, joined in a process of fervently renewing their Jewish religious identity and observance. Traditional Judaism which the previous generations considered a relic of the past, was now being rediscovered and practiced with great enthusiasm, love and dedication.

The process of returning to traditional Jewish observation of reuniting with one's soul, was found to be a most rewarding experience of spiritual and communal growth, although it was not a simple task. Many assimilated, uninformed, or non-practicing Jews have an impression that observant Jews live in a very easy life-style in which many of their decisions are made for them. The reality is quite different. The structure of Jewish life does provide a framework for living which does give a meaningful quality to life. This structure, however, in no way serves to absolve life from its difficulties and challenges. In fact, for Jews who have chosen to be observant of Jewish law, there are numerous additional conflicts and difficulties which beset them.

The religious mind functions within the framework of certain absolutes. There are limits to what is right and what is not right. In the secular framework, there are very few set limits or absolutes. The secular mind tends to see everything as being right as long as one is not overly offended by it. It becomes easy for the skeptic to criticize observing Jews, and to point out inconsistencies in their behavior. The observing Jew risks being called a hypocrite while trying to live up to an ideal. It is far more difficult for non-observing Jews to be called hypocrites since there are few, if any, standards for which they are obliged to uphold.

Besides the widely documented issues of Jews being ridiculed and hated by members of other religions, a religious Jew is typically seen as being emotionally upsetting to a non-religious Jew. Non-observant Jews often feel uncomfortable if not somewhat guilty when in the presence of an observing Jew. In response to these feelings, non-observant Jew's may assume an offensive position in support of their own lack of Jewish affiliation, knowledge, and participation. The non-observant Jew's life. Often the religious Jew is put on the defensive to justify his or her religious faith. When questioned the religious Jew is expected to produce total explanation for the entire religious system of Judaism along with justifying all of its difficult-to-understand precepts in ten words or less. This Jew is also expected to explain why bad things happen to good people along with why there are some religious people who do evil acts.

As this complex explanation is attempted, a common experience is that within moments, the listener is turning away his or her head with an expression of boredom and ludicrousness. This most difficult task of justifying one's ways tends to leave the religious Jew in the status of not only being misunderstand but being dismissed as a mentally archaic aberration. The Jew who takes his religion seriously often has to stand alone when being ridiculed and is subjected to belittling remarks by the secular mind.

Secular or non-traditional Jewish families go through great pain having to deal with a child who now decides to become observant of Jewish life. The family members are often confronted with confusion and, in many cases, feelings of guilt for neglecting their own Jewish observance and education. Secularized parents have been known to respond to their religious child in frustration by saying, "Why can't you remain like you used to be?"

Due to Jewish dietary laws, the child can no longer eat in the parent's non-kosher home or go out to a restaurant which does not serve Kosher food. Whereas the parents, siblings, and/or friends generally went out to a party, a show, or a sporting event on a Friday night or shopping on Saturday afternoon, the one now observing the Shabbat cannot participate in such activities. Life for the observant Jew stands out in contrast to the non-observant Jew. These differences can create frustration and strained relations among family members.

Dating becomes additionally difficult for the observant Jew. In dating for the purpose of marriage, the observant Jew is confronted with the problem of finding a mate who will be understanding and sympathetic to the practice of a traditional Jewish life style. The complexities of finding a fitting Jewish mate are difficult enough for a non-observant Jew, especially for a Jew who lives outside of a major Jewish community. All the more so it is difficult for the observant Jew who is not only restricted to the marriageable age Jewish population but also to that population which would be willing to live a devoted and committed Jewish life style.

An observant Jewish home has a number of emphasized qualities which would likely be seen as peculiar to the non-observant or uninformed. The concept of giving charity is highly valued in the observant home. These considerations make the process of mate selection confined to a limited population. To assist with this situation, there are dating services specializing in match making for the observant Jew. Social retreats attracting several hundred observant single Jews are planned at resort hotels in the east. These expensive weekends are tailored to assist in the match making procedure. Many people attend these retreats with the hope that they will meet their future mate. There are a number of success stories, but there are many more young adults who leave these retreats feeling even more alone.

Jews who choose to live a traditional Jewish life style are blessed with many gifts of happiness, warmth, and beauty. Yet, as described above, there are many issues in which the observant Jew differs from the rest of society. Due to these experiences, observant Jews may often find themselves in a position of standing alone and being criticized for their attitude of spiritual quest.

The observant Jew is clear in his or her position as to what they desire to achieve for the world. Their wish is that through living a particular tradition, they will be helping to make the earth a better place. The religious person strives to bring a greater degree of harmony into a world of dissonance. The religious personality desires to sanctify the mundane, bring life to that which is depressed, help people achieve higher levels of completeness and perfection, and work towards bringing humankind together as one.

In the face of predictions which claimed that observant Judaism would virtually come to a halt within the next generation, there has been a surprising turn-around taking place. Although the movements of assimilation and secularization continue to be very strong, cults from Scientology to Reverend Moon continue to invest large sums of money to actively recruit Jewish prey. There is a fervent group of Jews who are in touch with the concept of "returning," to identify and unite with the Jewish soul. These people have chosen to plant new seeds for the continued rebirth of traditional Jewish life. It is important to point out that this traditional Jewish life does differ from that of the past generations. The modern observant Jew is not only traditional in his or her life style, but is also a conservant contributor within today's modern, technically sophisticated era.

In spite of the many difficulties, the religious personality is typically imbued with meaning and purpose. In this case, the soul is not in a state of being "missing," but is in a position of being nurtured, challenged and spiritually renewed on an ongoing basis.

Judaism and Jungian Psychology:
A Personal Experience
J. Marvin Spiegelman, Ph.D.

The following is a case-study of "A Modern Jew in Search of Soul." The case is that of myself, although I shall be summoning up experiences of others and making generalizations which may have a larger application. How can I dare do this? How can one be so foolhardy or self-centered as to use his own experiences, particularly those of an inner life, to describe such a collective condition as the contemporary Jew coming to terms with his Jewishness and himself? In a typically Jewish fashion, I shall answer that question with a question: how else can one do it? Are we not all encased within our own psyches, bounded not only by an impinging environment, but also by the heredity which we bring to life? Our individuality, both potential and actualized, results from an interaction between the "given" and the "possible," as my favorite Dutch Protestant theologian Gerhard van der Leew put it.[1] We are born into or "given" time, place, family, tribe, etc., but we are also free to develop, to change, to combine, those "givens" in new possibilities or wholes. In short, I am presenting my personal myth, as Jung called it.

Another piece of my personal myth (not the Jewish part) was included in a book written by my friend and colleague, Mokusen Miyuki, and myself, called *Buddhism and Jungian Psychology*.[2] Towards the end of writing that book, I was visited by a bad conscience: Why was I not writing about Jungian psychology and my own tradition, Judaism? As I sweated this question and was resolving to do such a book, my publisher asked me to participate in this present book, *A Modern Jew in Search of Soul*. The synchronicity seemed meaningful and precise: I should continue with this explication of my personal myth, since the network of lines of fate, the force field of events, was welcoming it. So here it is.

What is that strange myth that has a Jew writing about himself in the context of Jungian Psychology and Buddhism, and then Judaism and Jungian Psychology? Is he a Japanese Jew? No, not quite. But, in the second year of his analysis, at the age of twenty-five, he had a big dream and a vision at Christmas time in which he witnessed the birth of a divine child–not an already born one, such as Jesus–but a new one. Three new "kings" or wise men were there to welcome the birth of this child and to nourish its development. These kings were a Jewish rabbi, a Christian priest, and a Buddhist priest. So, then, in a not atypical Jungian fashion, part of my myth has been ecumenical. In order to develop that representation of divine wholeness in my Self, I have needed to pursue deeply both a Christian and a Buddhist strand in my soul, as well as my basic Jewish core.

This ecumenical myth, as a matter of fact, is not so strange after all. I have met more than one person, of different religious and ethnic background, who has been similarly propelled. I reported a dream of such a person, which foresaw a religious structure of the future incorporating all of the triad of my own myth plus others, in my paper on "Psychotherapy and the Clergy: Fifty Years later."[3] All of us, furthermore, who have read Jung's *Memoirs*[4] remember his profound experience in his seventies, when he dreamed ecumenically on three successive nights. He experienced the exaltation of the Jewish image of Kabbalistic union of Malkuth with Tifereth, the Christian Marriage of the Lamb, and the pagan Greek *hierosgamos* (p. 294). Indeed, I think that my myth, like Jung's, is an individuation story.

This ecumenical myth, with its historical roots, seems to be afoot generally. Many of us need to not only find and buttress our uniqueness, but also to link ourselves with the rest of humankind. Only in such a way can we build that more complete future for which we long. Even as I formulate this longing, I hear the Jewish voice speaking, the echo of the religious prophets of the past, of Moses and Isaiah, and of even that benighted and anti-semitic Jewish prophet of the last century, Karl Marx, who also longed for a future paradise, an anti-utopian utopia, in which heave comes to earth and we are redeemed in community.[5] Jung, too, I think, is part of this prophetic tradition, and we even draw our very title from him, *Modern Man in Search of a Soul*. The conclusion he draws, of the need to strengthen the individual against atomization and collectivization, is one strand in the dilemma of individuality and community.

I return, now, to my personal story. I was born into the Jewish community of East Los Angeles in 1926 to a mother who immigrated from England as an infant and a father who came from Poland in his late teens. All my grandparents were from Poland, city and village, forest and *shtetl*. My parents were social democrats, American-loving and eager to move away from the poverty and religious rigidity of their origins. My paternal grandparents, who arrived in the United States only shortly before I was born, when my grandfather was already seventy, belonged to the past–they were wholly orthodox, religious, and closer to the Middle Ages than the Twentieth century. My grandfather, particularly, seemed like Moses with his white beard, deep blue eyes, imposing patriarchal manner, husband of two women (sequentially) and father of many children. He was an important figure to me, about which I shall have much to say presently.

The general theme of this family, however, like so many others, was the maintenance of family ties, of kinship, of survival and advancement beyond poverty, of social justice and service. The strands of Americanization, socialist ideology, hope for Israel, etc., were much like those of other Jewish families who immigrated from Eastern Europe to find new life in the Promised Land of America. They often tended to lose their deeply religious and community-oriented philosophy, and to embrace new images of redemption. I have used this kind of material, fictionalized, in my story of Julia, the Atheist-Communist, in my book, *The Trees: Tales in Psychomythology*.[7] I shall refer more fully to these stories later on, but here, suffice it to say that the image of *Haskala*, of the Jews of the *shtetl* and the enclosed community of the faithful leaving it and joining the world, was the theme therein. The world was discovered but God got lost.

Not so for my grandfather, I hasten to add, who provided a physical link with tradition for me, and in the years of my first analysis, served as a symbol for that link spiritually.

The Jewish content of my life as a child was not particularly profound nor complete. There was the gastronomic Jewishness of traditional Friday night dinners and Sunday breakfasts of bagels, cream cheese and lox. There was the observance of certain festivals at my grandparent's house: Passover, the High Holidays. In that sense, there was a celebration of kinship and community, but of religious content, only a little. What I did recall of the divine element, was visiting my grandfather in temple during the High Holidays. The old men would gather in the basement of the synagogue during the day and there was serious "davvening". In the swaying and intensity of the old men, their religious fervor was apparent. They were different from the members of the upper gallery for whom fine clothes and appearance carried more weight. I suspect that many of my generation will recognize some of their own experience in what I describe here.

But there was Jewish education as well for me and my fellow young males, but not much for the females. We went to Hebrew school for several years, but of the socialist Workmen's Circle type. We studied Yiddish, reading and writing, but not enough Hebrew to really use it, and little of the Bible. These thrice-weekly after-school sessions, however, were often missed, fought against and derided by my young ruffian friends and myself. Better to play handball against garages nearby, than attend the boring classes. Poor Mr. Perlmutter, our teacher, and how unkind we were to him! Jews with no soul might have been his judgement of us, indeed, and with right.

All that changed when we were in "basic training" for the bar-mitzvah, however. Now there were serious things to learn: the prayers, commentaries, the particular portion to read, the speech to be written and memorized. Now, perhaps, the religious sense began playing a role. We had to submit to discipline, to an initiation into adulthood (at thirteen?–our ancestors were more mature, to be sure). There began to be some link between the private experiences of God that I had as a child and these events, but the connection was vague and not a source of significant conflict or importance. There was such a thing as being Jewish, important as much for the minority aspect as anything else, but this was different from those experiences of the soul which a later self would describe as numinous, as tinged with awe and wonder. Jewish life was social life, except for *Zaideh*, my grandfather, who carried both.

I would say, then, that my Jewish religious life, was essentially lacking until I began my own analysis at the age of twenty-four with a German-Jewish survivor of the concentration camps, Dr. Max Zeller. Here was an educated, cultured man who was also religious! This was rare among the teachers and professors I had known. Besides this incongruity, I had the shock of my life within a few months of beginning my analytic work. I had completed my first Active Imagination, a work with fantasy in which the person continues a kind of dialogue with dream figures. This active fantasy included some water-color paintings and a description of a relationship with an unknown female dancer. It was called "Purple in the Blue." I brought it to my analytic session and, in the waiting room, I happened to look at some books of the *Zohar*,[8] which had just arrived. Opening one of the volumes at random, I read material which was very much like what I had written in my own fantasy! Trembling, I went upstairs to report this event to my analyst and was so struck by this synchronicity, that it took me sixteen years to really look a these books again. I had to study all sorts of other mysticism and religious experience before I had the courage to return. Only later did I discover that it was also part of that same Jewish mystical tradition that one should not undertake Kabbalistic study until the age of forty. So, I was a proper Jewish pupil after all!

As a "A Modern Jew in Search of Soul," I had found within myself an undeniable and uncanny link with my Jewish heritage, that was to permanently change my direction. At the same time, I had dreams about my grandfather and felt a longing to speak with him more fully about the family, the past, and Jewish matters. I therefore supplemented my analytic sessions with frequent visits to my grandparents, where I was cordially received. This was in 1951, the last year of his life, when he was in his ninety-seventh year. My grandmother, too, surely fulfilled for me the archetypal Great Mother with her kindness, humor and goodwill. She, also lived into her nineties.

Even now, as I write, I recall those visits with emotion. And I also recall the equally profound event of an earlier time, when I was eighteen, in the Merchant Marine, and about to go on a war-time voyage around the world. My grandfather, when he saw me in my cadet-midshipman's uniform, gave me a blessing. It was a blessing, of course, for a safe-journey, but it was also, as I later learned and experienced, a blessing in the ancient sense, like that of Jacob by his father Isaac. I was deeply moved by this event, and felt it most profoundly. I knew that I had to continue the family spirit in some way, and carry on that which my grandfather had valued so highly. I, too, like the Biblical Jacob, was not the oldest grandchild, but felt singled out. This was in harmony with my religious experience as a very young child in which I felt a specialness of connection with the God above (associated with the sun). So, now, my Jewish vocation was anchored, not only by the blessing of my grandfather, but by the psychic events of my early analysis. A modern Jew was in search of his soul, indeed.

There was no more particularly Jewish content in my analytic work for the next two or so years, although there were themes, such as the flood, which hearkened back to Biblical events. I also profited very much from attending seminars on a Jungian view of certain Biblical tales, provided, for example, by the visiting Swiss-Jewish Jungian Analyst, Rivkah Scharf-Kluger.[9] She also gave a deeply affecting seminar on the as-yet-untranslated book of Jung, *Answer to Job*.[10] That book was to have a great influence upon me, and is, I think, one of his most important contributions, particularly to Jews and to those of us who are both deeply committed to our origins and alive to the changes the soul is undergoing. I shall have more to say about this later on. At present, however, I wish to return to the final strikingly Jewish event to occur during my first analysis. Once more this involves my grandfather, although he had died two years earlier.

It was the fall of 1953. I was about to complete my analysis, and was facing a call-up into military service within a few months. It was during the Korean War, in which I was to serve for two years as an Army Psychologist. Also, I was about to get married. One night, thinking about these things, and also wondering what to do in the way of ritual for my forthcoming marriage, I went to the La Brea Tar Pits park, a place that I had frequented when I lived in that area from ages ten to eighteen. In 1953, it was still an oasis of solitude in the midst of the surrounding city, and I sat upon a bench in quiet reflection. All at once, I felt my grandfather present, not as a ghost, but as a quality of personality. Without words, he suggested/ordered me to stand up and walk. Without cavil, I did so, and began a walk up Fairfax boulevard, towards the Jewish community district. After a few blocks, my grandfather directed me to cross the street and go into a building. It was not until I was close to the building that I recognized it as a synagogue. Opening the door–it was a Friday night–I saw ahead of me, praying and speaking to an assembled congregation, a man who looked remarkably like my grandfather. He was tall, white bearded, strong-faced, and he "davvened" with great intensity.

I knew at once that this was the rabbi that my grandfather wanted to conduct the marriage ceremony. After the service, I went up to him and learned that he was named Rabbi Jacob (like my grandfather!) Sonderling. He said that he would happy to perform the ceremony for us, but would like to meet with us first. I was delighted and, when we chatted a little, was surprised to discover that he had a Ph.D. (just as I had received the year before), but in philosophy, not psychology. He studied the psychology of aesthetics, however, and had been a pupil of Ebbinghaus, no less. This seemed synchronistic, to be sure, and I thanked my grandfather, inwardly, for directing me to such a fine and kind gentleman. The synchronicity did not end at that point, however.

When my bride-to-be met with Rabbi Sonderling, it emerged that he had known her paternal grandfather in Europe during World War I. Rabbi Sonderling was a rabbi in the German army, at the time, and was touring the border areas of Poland on behalf of the German Jewish community, to assist the *shtetls* with what they might need. Rabbi Sonderling was particularly impressed by my wife's grandfather, Rabbi Silberstein, in that he asked only that his community continue to be able to honor the Sabbath totally, rather than serve German soldiers on that day. Piety over profit, even for impoverished Jews, was an impressive value. This link, then, with the grandfathers of my wife and myself was very moving to us. The wedding ceremony was one that we will never forget. The power of it made it clear to me that whatever one's inner religious experience, it is essential that certain collective events always belong with the community, and that the psyche itself longs for this. As I was also to realize later on with the births of my children, all these turning-point events required collective celebration and ritual. I would say, therefore, that birth, initiation, marriage and death are the minimum four passages to be so fulfilled. It is in this sense that I agree with one derivation of the word religio as "linking back." It is linking with God in community and tradition.

How, then, is one to understand these powerful Jewish impressions from my early analysis and at its conclusion? Why did it happen this way and what was my psyche trying to communicate to me? I think that these psychological events were "timed," as it were. Whenever there is a concatenation of an inner condition and an outer meaningful event, as Jung termed synchronicity, strong emotions are present. When, in addition, these synchronistic events, with their archetypal connection, also touch upon collective rituals, celebrations and "sacred time" (as Eliade calls it[11]), an especially large quantum of psychic energy is released. It has been especially noteworthy for me with Jewish events, but they have also occurred at moments sacred to Christian and Buddhist tradition. For example, my fundamental myth experience of the three kings or priests took place precisely at Christmas time; and my experience of speaking in Tokyo on East and West occurred not only at the time of Buddha's birthday, but along with me on the podium were both Buddhist and Christian priests!

This, the, is one link between the ongoing psychological or inner experience of a religious nature, so fully described by Jung, and that of community tradition. Jung has preferred the derivation of *religio* as "careful observation of the numinous," which associates it more with individual experience. My inner or psychologically observed religious experiences have been quite frequent, if not ongoing, although their link with community has been relatively rare, but profound. I believe, than, that my psyche was providing itself both a base and an outer connection during this first experience of my analytic youth, so to speak, and this was necessary to support the requirement of standing alone, of which Jung speaks. In short, I really needed to know who I was, both personally and collectively, before I could truly embrace my utter particularity later in life.

Such a necessity to stand alone did occur later in life, when I was forty, and that, too involved the image of my grandfather. One spring afternoon, after a totally frustrating experience of injustice on the part of senior Jungian colleagues, I decided to resign my membership in the local society. As I drove home in tears, I experienced deeply what I felt like utter betrayal at the hands of my analytical fathers. This was in marked contrast to my own father, who had always been a source of warmth and emotional support. As I crossed the mountain pass on the way to my home, I had a vision of my grandfather, once more, and Jung, both of whom came forward to embrace me. There was love and joy in their faces as they pulled me to them. At the next moment, the three were dancing a *hora* which felt like the ecstatic celebrations of the *hasidim*. I knew, then, that I was connected, inwardly, to the Jewish heritage, as represented by my grandfather, and to the spirit of my own individuation as represented by Jung. Yet there was an inner similarity between Jung and my grandfather. When I completed my studies in Switzerland, I felt the need to see Jung alone and to receive his blessing in some way, as a prelude to doing analytic work. I had passed the requirements, but the image of the blessing was strong for me, just as it had been when my grandfather blessed me when I went off to war. Jung obliged me, in our session, which I have described elsewhere.[12] Suffice to say here that he, too, gave me a link with God, by his being, by his manner of relating and by example.

Since that time of the "hora" with Jung and my grandfather, the latter's image has no longer appeared as such, but there have been variants of the archetype behind my experience of him in much of my fictional writing. Indeed, it was only after that separation/individuation from my local society that my particular brand of fictional writing, psycho-mythology, began.

From that time onwards, my Jewish experiences–of an inner nature, at least–have lost much of their particularity and have blended in with the totality of my myth. For example, in the *The Tree*,[13] there are three specifically Jewish story-tellers out of ten. That is a "minyan" of five men and five women, each of whom represents a different religion, belief system or attitude, but all carrying out their own individuation. Of the three Jews included, on is a Knight.[14] His story, of the fragmentation of the divine and the need of God for humanity in order to be whole, is connected with the Jewish gnosticism. A second Jew is Julia, the Atheist-Communist, whom I mentioned before, and a third is the Medium, Sophie-Sarah. The latter examines the Holocaust from a Kabbalistic point-of-view. Jewish elements appear in other parts of the ten tales, as they also do in the sequels to the first book, *The Quest*[15] and *The Love*.[16] These as I say, are blended, so that in the inner realm, at least, they constitute parts of the totality.

Inner blending did not result in an integrated connection to religious community, however. An understanding of this failure was made clearer to me from a dream I had at the time of my son's bar-mitzvah. Several years before this event, our family joined an orthodox synagogue and I participated in this process of my son's education by going to Saturday services with him and by having frequent discussions with the rabbi. I even spent some time examining a Jewish mystical text together with him. The night before the day of my son's ritual initiation, however, and in the full flush of excitement and preparation, I dreamed as follows:

> I am in a room adjacent to the synagogue. It is like the study room in which I had the discussions with the rabbi, but also has the quality of the sacristy in Catholic churches, where the priest dresses for the service. In this room, I am at first looking through drawers, trying to find a white dress shirt which fits me. Preparations are going on next door for the bar-mitzvah and the regular Saturday service and I am afraid I will be late. I search for a shirt, but they are all too small. I notice that some of them belong to the father of my son's friend, a man who is in no way psychological and is quite content to be a member of the congregation. But his shirts don't fit me. I start to get a bit frantic, especially when I notice that there is also present a German-Jewish acquaintance who is a woman particularly finicky about doing things according to the rules. Her disapproval of my clothes also bothers me. I shrug my shoulders, however, and gesture to her my incapacity to find the right shirt and my apology therefore. At that moment, she vanishes, and I am, instead, with the rabbi. We look at each other, but a recognition of our differences also. We then look up at the ceiling of the room, which has a silk covering. This silk is very beautiful, but there is a large rent in it. As the rabbi and I look at this torn silk covering, we nod, as if we understand that the "fabric," meaning the fabric of Jewish wholeness, is torn. He and I are together, however, and my son, next door, will be undergoing his bar-mitzvah alone, but with God. As the dream ends, I hear my son chanting with great feeling and joy as he concludes the prayers. I am relieved that he can do it for himself.

The dream, I think, requires no interpretation, but only comment. In point in fact, it was and is difficult for me to be a member of a congregation: I don't have the right *persona* for it, in Jung's sense, or the social know-how. I always am moved and deepened by the services, but find the institutional obligations onerous. Nor can I satisfy the requirements of fitting in with the proper rules. That is certainly my own inadequacy. The dream says, however, that there is also a rent in the fabric of Jewish existence. Ever since the destruction of the Temple, that tornness is felt in the endless persecutions in the diaspora, and the present division in Jewish life (as in my stories), among the orthodoxy observant, the "protestant reformation" (Conservative, Reform, and Reconstructionist Judaism), and the "socialist," "individualist" or "humanist" Jews who embrace *Haskala*. There are people, like myself, furthermore, who are deeply religious inwardly, but who can belong to none of these sects of the larger Jewish community–or any other for that matter–but feel akin to all of them. Our condition is like the Modern Man that Jung referred to. He was speaking of the European who was both Protestant and Catholic and could easily see the values and limitations of each. He had hope for the European of the future, therefore, who was inwardly both.

Jung himself, however, was something other as well. I have already referred to the great dream of his seventies, in which he experienced the heights of the three divine Jewish, Christian and pagan Greek images. Do I delude myself to averring that my own experiences also move in that direction? Obviously, I think not. And I would add that there is no doubt whatsoever that my deep commitment in this life is to my Jewish "given" and I still work on finding a way to connect that inner multiplicity to some outer Jewish vessel, which this book symbolizes.

For many years that vessel has been provided by a familial celebration of holidays at our own "temple," our home. This, of course, is itself a deeply Jewish tenet: the home and family, not synagogue, is at the center of Jewish observance. In the last few years, however,

I have also been attending High Holiday services under the leadership of my friend and former pupil, Rabbi Levi Meier, who is also a contributor to this book. The gift to my soul, that my family and friends can attend these services, and that my son plays the *shofar*, is an indication that it is possible to unite inner and outer, at least at times. In the synchronicity of time, even this book–to which several Jews of different stripe contribute–indicates this possibility of a congregation of the spirit. All of us have experienced the rending, the endurance of which may be necessary until our wholeness is born from the struggle.

That now brings me to some transpersonal considerations. I belong to that group of "individual" Jews, who constitute one branch of the modern Jewish condition. Others, as in my stories, are the socialist/social democrats, the religiously observant, the ethnic Jews of various stripes, among others. Indeed, one can say that of the Jews who have survived the Holocaust and world persecution, there are still "three opinions for each two Jews," yet all of them can find a psychological space in the modern state of Israel. Even those extreme religious Jews who reject statehood until the coming of the Messiah can fin a home there. Indeed, the modern symbol for Jewish lie and existence is Israel itself. It is the one commonality which is defended by almost all of us and looked upon with great emotion. Some have even said that Israel has taken the place of God for the contemporary Jew! As a symbol, that may be true, although one would have to add that the state is a manifestation of the earthing of the ancient image of return.

From a psychological point-of-view, I want to mention just three themes which I find are central in the spiritual dimension of Jewish life. The first of these is the question of the clash of certain opposites, such as individual vs. community, full Torah observance vs. flexibility. A spokesperson of the Halachic way of life is to be found in the inspired writing of Rabbi Joseph Soloveitchik, whose *Halachic Man*[17] and "Lonely Man of Faith"[18] are marvels of the expression of the traditional way of life, enlivened by clarity of vision and eloquence of faith. A person reading such work wants to immediately wear phylacteries and live an observant life. From him one can realize that all life is sacred and that the living of the *mitzvot* is an ideal way to manifest the divine in everyday human existence.

Yet there is a rent in Jewish existence and it will continue–as the ultra–orthodox agree–until the Messiah comes. From a psychological point-of-view that redemption can also appear inwardly, with the individual. It does show itself sometimes with those of us who work deeply with souls of seekers. That separation also shows itself, outwardly and inwardly, I believe, by the changing attitude towards the feminine and women in modern life generally. There is no doubt that the Crown of Kabbalah must unite with his feminine counterpart, Shekinah, here in life, that God must be whole in a masculine and feminine way. This union needs to appear both in the soul and in community. The issue begins to be joined by some women, such as Gloria Feman Orenstein, Ph.D., and there is representation of such seeking in the present volume. My own view is that the Kabbalistic tradition of Jewish mysticism, as a counter-pole to the *Halachic* observance of Rabbi Soloveitchik, provides a key.

Yet much of what changes in Jewish life and belief will be wrought as a result of the women's movement and must come from women themselves. As I write these words, I come into possession of a dream from a modern Jewish woman, who has little religious education, but in middle life finds a need for an outer realization and connection with inner experiences. She dreams as follows:

> I am in the newly rebuilt synagogue at B Temple. It is simple and clean, white and airy with a raised ceiling and small balcony. I must be sitting near the front. To my amazement, congregants are rising one by one and each person is describing the wound of his early childhood. Each statement is precise and clear, using Kleinian, Jungian and Freudian vernacular. People rise and speak from all over the Temple. I am awe struck. The consciousness I have been searching for is here in this newly constructed Temple. Is my function as a witness or are these voices aspects of me? I do not see myself speak yet. Maybe the Rabbi is present.

As with my own dream, I will here comment rather than interpret. This rebuilt Temple does not yet exist. In our dreamer's case, there is a combination of a psychological attitude and a religious one. Notably, the sects in the depth psychological tradition are now able to be unified within a religious vessel, and each individual carries weight and importance. At long last, the Temple becomes a true place for the soul and community. But the dreamer, a woman both modern and conscious, does not yet speak. The voice of women, of the feminine, is not yet fully heard. This dream, like my own, is ecumenical yet individual, religious and psychological, but both the new voice and the manifestation of the collective experience in the world is not yet ready. We can only be patient until this newer unity makes itself felt.

The more painful rift to be examined first, I believe, is the specter of growing assimilation on the part of Jews in the Diaspora. The threat to Jewish communities everywhere is compensated by the strength and vigor of Israel. From a psychological point of view, however, the issue is not only social and lack of Jewish education. As an analyst, I have seen Jewish patients who have needed very much to come to terms with Christian imagery and symbols, sometimes even coming close to being assimilated, in the sense of conversion. Usually this work leads to a deeper sense of appreciation of the "other" and the capacity to relate to it. Indeed, I think that the very psychological work done to grasp this "other" is what permits one to come to the deeper truths of one's self. I am more of a Jew myself, for example, for having had the necessity of connecting more deeply with the Christianity in my own soul. A great help in this inner and outer relationship to the attractive and oppressive "other" of Christianity, I believe, is the work of C.G. Jung. His book, *Answer to Job*,[19] in particular, provides an astonishing psychological history of the development of consciousness of the divine in our western tradition. It is the only work I know of that really can be said to be true to a "Judeo-Christian" continuity. Usually that word tastes bad in my mouth and is said as if one is combining an oriental martial art with Christianity. In Jung's case, however, every Jew can feel his confrontation with the image of God given to us. The resulting experience, of the wholeness of God, light and dark, masculine and feminine, which Jung's work leads to, is closer to our Jewish tradition than most of what Christian understanding has offered thus far.

In many ways, Jung approaches the Kabbalistic conception, but, apparently, it was only later that he learned fully what Jewish mysticism was about. In any case, I believe that this inner and outer confrontation becomes conscious of the damage that it has done to our people and soul. Certainly there are those in that community who are doing so. How many of us Jews, however, are prepared to take on an inner dialogue with the heretical God-Man? My own attempts[20] are satisfying to me, as are my continuing intimate relationships with committed Christians–and Buddhists–both in individual friendships and in a several-years-old-experiment called the "Psycho-Ecumenical Group." This gathering of people includes those who are simultaneously psychotherapists and members of the clergy: an orthodox rabbi, a Catholic priest, two nuns, an Episcopal priest, a Protestant minister, as well as a Buddhist priest and a layman (myself). We are well aware of these issues, and our continuing meeting makes me hopeful of the future for us all.

The three themes I have mentioned are capable of further emendation, but I want to close this presentation with a final dream, this time not my own but my father's. He, and many of his generation, did not consciously feel strongly about religion at all, and he still does not do so. Now, in his eighty-fifth year, *boruch ha-shem*, he still enjoys a zestful life and appreciation of an ethnic Judaism alone. Yet he dreamed some years ago, when he suffered a most rare incidence of illness, as follows.

> **He finds himself in the forests of his Polish boyhood, and is deeply affected by the intense green and the beauty. Then he is somewhere else in Europe and it is after the Holocaust. Everywhere he looks there is only destruction. Only small stones and bits of broken human objects are visible–a complete rubble. Then he sees only one thing that is undamaged: it is a stand upon which the Torah normally rests on the *bimah*. At that moment, he hears and then sees great numbers of youth, who are now coming to re-build once more. End of dream.**

Such a dream from a Jew who does not acknowledge religious sentiment is enough for us all. There is memory of beauty, there is the survival and rebirth of our people and there remains the carrier of our tradition and commitment, whether we choose it or not. This is because our chosenness is a "given," only to be reformulated in each new age and clime. My father has expressed it for us all. I am reminded of the story told by some famous European writer who heard that there were Jews who were not religious. He could not believe it, for the essence of the Jew, he thought, was the intense, personal and communal connection with God. This non-Jew understood us better than we understand ourselves.

NOTES

1. van der Leeuw, Gerhard, *Religion in Essence and Manifestation*, George Allen & Unwin Ltd, London, 1938 (original in 1933), 709 pp.
2. Spiegelman, J. Marvin and Miyuki, Mokusen, *Buddhism and Jungian Psychology*, Falcon Press, Phoenix, 1985.
3. Spiegelman, J. Marvin, "Psychotherapy and the Clergy: Fifty Years later," *Journal of Religion and Health*, Vol. 23, #1, 1984, pp. 19-32.
4. Jung, C.G., *Memories, Dreams, Reflections*, Pantheon Books, Random House, New York, 1961. 398 pp.
5. Spiegelman, J. Marvin, *Essay on Utopia*, on file at C.G. Jung Institute in Zurich, Switzerland, Chicago, Illinois and Los Angeles, California. 1958. 198 pp.
6. Jung, C.G., *Modern Man in Search of a Soul*, Kegan Paul, London, 1933.
7. Spiegelman, J. Marvin. *The Tree: Tales in Psycho-mythology*, Phoenix House, Los Angeles, 1975. Reprinted in paper-back by Falcon Press, Phoenix, 1982.
8. H. Sperling, translator, *The Zohar*, in five volumes. Soncino Press, London, 1933.
9. Kluger, Rivkah Schaerf, *Psyche and Bible*, Spring Publications, Zurich, 1974, 144 pp.
10. Jung, C.G. *Answer to Job*, Collected Works, Vol. 11, Original 1952.
11. Eliade, Mircea, *The Myth of the Eternal Return*, Routledge and Kegan Paul, London, 1955. 195 pp.
12. Spiegelman, J. Marvin, "Remembrance of Jung" in Jensen, F., Editor, *C.G. Jung, Emma Jung and Toni Wolff: Collection of Remembrances*, Analytical Psychology Club of San Francisco, 1982, pp. 86-89.
13. See note number 7.
14. One might ask how can a Knight be Jewish? And I would answer, in Passover fashion, that this is how this Knight differs from all other Knights!
15. Spiegelman, J. Marvin, *The Quest: Further Tales in Psycho-mythology*, Falcon Press, Phoenix, 1984, 175 plus x pp.
16. Spiegelman, J. Marvin, *The Love*, to be published in 1986-7.
17. Soloveitchik, Rabbi Joseph B., *Halakhic Man*, Jewish Publication Society of America, Philadelphia, 1983, pp. 164.
18. Soloveitchik, Rabbi Joseph B., "The Lonely Man of Faith," *Tradition*, Summer 1965, 5, 5-67.
19. See note 10.
20. In my psychomythological tales in *The Tree* and *The Quest* and most particularly in The Love.

Echad

Robert E. Bosnak, J.D.

I am a Dutch Jew who owes his life to Adolf Hitler.

When my parents married in 1936 it became clear that they could not have children. They went to several doctors in Holland but the verdict was final: it would not work. Thus, when the war broke out in 1940 they had no children. Rotterham, where they lived, was bombed flat. I remember parts of the left-over ruins when I grew up, bicycling to school. In 1942, the morning the razzias started in Rotterdam–they had already been in full swing in Amsterdam–they tore the star of David off their clothes and fled to Switzerland. Miraculously they came through. Five percent did, at that time. Then in a displaced person's camp in Switzerland my mother gave birth to my brother after having undergone an operation in a Swiss hospital that had been unknown in Holland. "I owe him to you," my mother said to the Swiss surgeon proudly holding up my brother to him. "I'm quite unaware of that," he is said to have answered dryly. To a Swiss doctor, yes. But to a Swiss doctor by the force of Adolf Hitler. This story gives me a chuckle of spite towards Hitler and a total bewilderment as to the designs of our God.

Our births and the birth of my entire generation of Dutch Jewish post-war babies, were miracles to our parents. Our bar mitzwahs, next to being as "Goodbye Columbus" as in the United States, were unconscious celebrations to the mysteries of survival. At the same time that we were miracles to our parents, we lived on top of a dark secret that was never spoken about. A secret filled with names of deceased relatives. At six I decided that I never wanted to know the secret and entered the unspoken conspiracy.

I was born between Auschwitz and Sinai, and so is each Jew of my generation.

Adonai Echad.

This is the credo of Hebrew Law. It means: Lord One. I was always told that this meant that there is only one God. Our God. So in my days of rebellion and anti-imperialist sentiment I abandoned him. I became an analyst and realized there were many Gods. But then he began to come back, this Adonai Echad of my Bar Mitzwa days. But somehow differently. Now he had become the Echad God, the one who suffers His undividable nature. The God of both Auschwitz and Sinai, the miracle and the unspeakable secret. Now I have this God whom I both despise from the bottom of my soul with a passion that amazes me and a God who I adore with equal fervor. I'm astonished and puzzled as when I was a kid and lived the torment of Echad.

Both Freud and Jung concentrated their studies on the dark conspiracy and the forces of love, the one calling them Thanatos and Eros, the other Shadow and Mysterium Coniunctionis, (the mystery of divine marriage). They each searched the well springs of darkness and light into the depth of Soul, Shechina. It can not be coincidental that psychoanalysis was founded in the souls of women. According to tradition, Shechina is the wife of Echad who suffers his passions on earth. His beloved. Shechina is the cosmos as it is actually lived on this earth.

In a dream practicum a woman told the following dream:

I am walking through a long dark tunnel. It reminds me of the terrible time I have gone through. Before me I see a huge door. Light comes from under the door. Then the door opens. A bright white light shines behind the huge door. The light is completely formless. I wake up.

I ask the dreamer to describe the tunnel as carefully as she can, directly from memory. She begins to tell about the walls she can underneath and the walls to her side. As she describes her memory of the dream, she slowly begins to inhabit the memory more and more till it is as if she is back in the dream of two nights ago. When I feel her fully present in the memory image–the more a person is present in a memory image of a dream, the more this image feels like a space the dreamer inhabits while she speaks–I ask here to have the dream unfold again. She looks around and sees the dark tunnel. Then she suddenly becomes aware of the light over the threshold under the gigantic door. She focuses on the door. It seems to be made out of wood. She goes clear to the door. She comes very close to the door when it suddenly opens. She stands back in awe. The light seems to be entirely behind the door; it does not really enter the darkness. I ask her if she can go a little more forward. She says that as she stretches her arm into the white light her arm will disapear: "Nothing can have form in the white light. My body is becoming very hot." I ask her to feel it. "The darkness behind me is cool. I can feel a red line going vertically through my body where the light and the darkness come together. The red line is cringing and squirming like a vein. "She begins to hyperventilate. "I am scared," she exclaims. "The red vein is tormented. I want to stop." Slowly I ask her to move away from this tormenting interface between light and dark. We breathe deeply together for a minute, till she begins to calm down. "I was really frightened," she says.

Jung, following the alchemists, called soul *Anima Media Natura*. The *Soul* in *the Middle between* opposing *Natures*. She is the medium, the conductor of both light and darkness, bond between formless eternal light and the darkness, bond between formless eternal light and the darkness of earth and underworld.

The alchemists saw this Soul embodied in the element Mercury, who consists of the double nature of fluidity and firmness, water and the metal silver. He was seen as hermaphroditical, both male and female. From this medium the alchemist eventually had to extract the remedy against ills, the *pharmacon*.

The word *pharmacon* means at the same time poison and medicine. It is not a product with two sides, like the two sides of the same coin, but it is the actual identity of poison and medicine. The identity of the miracle and the dark secret. Mercury is the carrier of identity in alchemy as Echad is the carrier of identity to the tribe of Judah.

The alchemists say that Mercury is chased from one bridal suite to the next in endless torment. He attaches herself to each and every material and thereby changes the shape of the material and her own shape. He subjects every form to his shape shifting and silver reflections. His fumes are deadly. What does that mean to the people of Echad?

I don't know.

I had one dream in analysis that returned time and again:

I see the little Warsaw boy with his cap over his forehead and his hands over his head. Behind him stand the German soldiers with their guns, laughing broadly. A voice tells me in Dutch: "All our old men have died. All the wise men are gone. Just the children are left behind. The children are bewildered."

I am alive and the little Warsaw boy has fallen anonymously into the dark secret. I want to strangle Echad like I want to knock the teeth out of the grinning German soldier. I live with the ones I love; children of my own. Miracle! I adore Echad.

The Search of A Swiss-Jewish-Israeli
Gustav Dreifuss, Ph.D.

When the editor of this book asked me to contribute a paper, he wrote that he would like to have "a Swiss-Jewish-Israeli" version of the theme. Well, I was born in Switzerland in 1921 to Jewish parents (traditional but not orthodox) and came to Israel in 1959 as an immigrant together with my wife and two little children. I have worked as a Jungian Analyst in Haifa ever since and I feel that my search of a soul will accompany me till the end of my days because the soul is living and transforming, renewing itself time and again.

Let me first play a bit with the words of the title: I leave out the word "modern" and then it says: *A Jew in search of a soul*. This is a different story. Has not every Jew, every man, a soul and therefore does he not have to search for it? A traditional believing Jew *has* his soul: he is connected with the spirit through his belief, through practicing his religion, through his connection with the rabbi and his community. A secular Jew may be in connection with the spirit by belonging to and identifying with a political party or with science, with progress.

Now I leave out the word Jew and replace it with man, then the title is as follows: *A modern man in search of a soul*. Here we are right in Jungian Psychology, the crisis of modern man, his not being contained in a religion, his *loss of soul*, of meaning in life. According to Jung, modern man has to find his roots within himself; he may then *experience* his soul in the process of his inner development; his numinous experience of the beyond will give him a sense of meaning and a feeling of taking part in the psychic and spiritual development of our time. Some of Jung's contributions to the crisis of our time are compiled in their English translation under the title: *Modern Man in Search of a Soul*. In the title of the book the word Man is replaced by Jew and the indefinite article "a" is added. I take this as meaning that the contribution of each author is expected to be a personal one. I am also a modern Jew in search of a soul, having become alienated from the traditional religion and looking for meaning, for soul, by looking inward, by relating to the unconscious, to the spirit within.

During my analysis from the end of 1940 until the middle of 1950, I had many religious dreams and some of them were connected with Israel. I will mention a few here:

15.11.49: I sit in front of a great large book in Hebrew letters. I have got the task to translate the book and to edit it.

23.1.50: I am in Israel and negotiate the purchase of large pieces of land. The price seems to me somewhat high.

4.5.51: I see many lorries full of books, on their way to Israel.

8.6.51: I fight, wrestle intensively, with the great man.

11.10.51: At the end of the day of atonement, the synagogue is almost empty. Mrs. X sits next to me, weeping. She says that she simply has no satisfaction in the synagogue and that this is terrible. I comfort her and say that one has to serve God in a different way.

25.2.55: I must mediate between Arabs and Jews.

15.7.55: I ride on a camel through the desert.

Without going into an interpretation of these dreams it becomes clear that *for me* Jewishness was related to Israel and it took me many years to come to the inner conviction that a central part of my Jewishness had to be expressed through my emigration from Switzerland to Israel. In other words, I gradually felt that at this point in my life, approaching the age of forty, it was not enough *for me* to under the dreams only symbolically and to search my Jewish soul by immersing myself in the study and psychological understanding of the Jewish scriptures while living in Switzerland. I had to give body, substance to my Jewish soul by dwelling in the land of the Bible of the Jewish past. I must add here that the experience of Nazism and of the holocaust and considerably added to my decision for Aliyah, for settling in Israel.

This brings me to yet another variation of the title: *A modern Israeli Jew in search of a soul.* Today I belong to this category.

Immigration to Israel and an individual way of relating to the Jewish scriptures and to actual problems of Israelis, i.e. Holocaust victims in psychological treatment have not stopped my process of soul searching, of inner development. Time and again I try to understand the Jewish fate of being persecuted, threatened, killed in the Diaspora as well as in Israel (wars, terrorism).

Living in Israel, I am very much concerned with the ongoing radicalization in Israel society. I miss tolerance from the different sections of our society. I am sad that the feeling of togetherness, of a common bond, is alive almost only in times of danger.

Already forty years ago I gave up any demands for spiritual leadership by the religious establishment and turned, with the help of Jungian psychology, to my soul for guidance. She, my soul, my anima, enables me to find an individual way of expressing my Jewishness. And I feel that this connection to the soul and the Jewish spirit helps me to become more human, more tolerant of my fellow men.

This morning, while meditating, I concentrated on the theme of this book and I would like to share some of the images that came up: First I saw before my inner eye an orthodox Jew moving his body rhythmically in prayer. I turned into his rhythm and felt the ever present energies of expansion and contraction, like the beating of the heart or in-and exhaling. Cosmic energy streamed through my body and I felt elated. This image was followed by the words "My God, my God, why hast Thou forsaken me?" (Psalm XII/2: Eli, Eli lama asavtani?) A feeling of loneliness, of sadness overcame me. I had no energy and felt cut off from the source of life. Moments of despair and suffering became real to me and brought forth the image of the Wailing Wall. This connected me to the destruction of the Temple, the dispersion of the Jewish people and its suffering throughout history. This was followed by images of the Holocaust, photographs, films and I remembered some of the victims of the Holocaust I had worked with in therapy during the last twenty-five years. I recalled details of their stories, the fear or lack of expression in their eyes while relating their experiences. I felt powerless as a human being in the face of fateful destructive forces. This depressive mood suddenly changed and I saw myself walking in the fields of the Emek, in the woods of the Carmel, along the sea and in the Old City of Jerusalem. I enjoyed nature, pregnant with memories of a distant past. The corn in the fields, the sheep and goats on the Carmel connected with the fertility of the land when properly cultivated and I was thankful to mother earth, to the goodness of Fertility, to the feminine principle, to the Shekhina. I was happy to have found the feminine principle alive in the Jewish scriptures, in the Kabbala.

And then came another association connected to the title of this book: A Jewish soul "a Yiddische Neschume". It expresses itself in a joyful and at the same time melancholic way. It is connected with the suffering Jew of Eastern Europe and also in the joy of Jewishness, of the Shabbat, of the Holidays. Paintings of Chagall rose before my inner eye as well as the story: Tevia, the Milkman. It is this Jewish soul which lives in all the Jews, yet has lost its impact on many Jews since the emancipation.

Summing up, I feel that my search of a soul was meaningful. The ups and downs of many years pass before me. The key-word of soul-searching for me is *patience*, so difficult to attain. I need it for myself and for my next of kin, for my friends and for my analysands. I feel that helping others individually in their soul-searching is my best contribution towards a possible transformation of the collective soul towards the year 2000, the new aeon.

An American in Jerusalem and The Search for Soul

By William Alex, M.D.

In the context of this discussion, search of a soul implies "loss of soul." It assumes that the modern Jew in question has either lost his/her soul or is in the process of losing it—whatever it may be. The soul, like the ancient Egyptian Ba or Ka, is a difficult entity to define. In Jewish theology it is the immortal part but not entirely separable from the body at death. In its personal form it is the invisible essence and animating or actuating principle in the individual's life. There are, to be sure, large numbers of modern Jews who are still contained and nourished by the traditional forms and contents of Judaism. There are also the *hozrim b'tchuva* who have strayed and are returning to the fold filled with *elan*, a contemporary phenomenon. My comments in this essay are directed not toward these contained individuals but to the mass of today's Jew who, like myself, have not found a resting place within traditional Judaism for a number of reasons, some of which I will touch upon here.

For me, a Jungian psychologist, soul or anima manifests in the individual as the subject's attitude toward his inner life; toward his dreams, fantasies, vague moody strivings, toward his thoughts, feelings and sensations which well up from the unconscious psyche. In it, is embodied his real inner sense of identity, often at variance with his outer adaptation, with the objective world, and as a rule, compensatory to it. A Jew living in our contemporary world, particularly one raised in a liberal, democratic tradition must, of necessity, accept a paradox and ambivalence as his daily fare. For such a Jew, loss of Jewish soul means the loss of his inner living connection and meaningful relationship to an ancient, three-thousand-year-old heritage, to an indefinable sense of being part of an ongoing historical and religious process whose contribution to world civilization, to its theology, ethics, laws, and to the overall growth of human consciousness is beyond reckoning.

As an American living in Jerusalem for the past decade, I find the subject at hand particularly complex, emotionally charged, and diverse, a convoluted entity involving a number of overlapping disciplines. And none of them is comprehensible with regard to Jewish existence apart from the whole. My comments will be personal for I claim no special expertise in Judaic matters. But I have been deeply and not unemotionally involved with the problems and fortunately the available literature on the subject is extensive and impressive. I will touch upon a few of the problematic and controversial contents that are troubling food for thought. Among these are: the impact of the holocaust on our image of God, the "who is a Jew" question, the dispute about the exclusive matrilinear Jewish descent, and the doctrine of the chosen people.

Let me first address myself to the main point. To avoid misunderstanding, I would like to stress that in my use of the term God, I specifically refer to our God-image. I will designate the unknowable metaphysical God concept when required and I beg the reader's indulgence if the distinction I intend between the two concepts appears less clear-cut than I would like it to be. I fully concur with R.L. Rubenstein who asserts in his book, *After Auschwitz* (1), "It is not possible to brutally rip out and liquidate one-third of a people without grave alterations and repercussions in the psyche of that people". He continues further, "Our image of God has been permanently impaired. No Jewish theology will possess even a remote degree of relevance to contemporary Jewish life if it ignores the question of God and the death camps."

For the Jew, as for the rest of mankind, the holocaust was an unmitigated disaster beyond the range of ordinary comprehension, for it uncovered in an ostensibly modern, highly cultured nation and conceivably in all of us–the potential for savagery and degradation unheard of previously. Rubenstein reflects that even to impose on the victims a sense of the tragic seems disrespectful, for tragedy conveys a sense of meaning–however grim. I submit that the holocaust offers no such comfort either to thought or feeling. All of it has come to reside within the range of human potential, and the realization is frightening.

Certain often repeated questions remain to haunt and plague us. Where was the traditional Jewish God when his chosen people were being exterminated like noxious insects? Why did this God display such hostility toward the descendants of Israel, the pious and innocent together with the sinful and assimilated? Why did the God of Israel permit–one could even say willfully use the Nazi death machine to reduce European Jewry to the status of social garbage? And what is there about the Jew and his traditional God-image, and consequently his way of life, that has with heartbreaking regularity throughout two thousand years of exile thrust him, until recently, into the role of passive, unresisting scapegoat subject to vicious insults, slander, sub-human projections and murderous violence culminating in the holocaust? I will return to this last question later.

Elie Weisel wrote, "I do not understand. I understand neither the killers nor their victims. The concentration camps elude the philosophers and also the novelists". I would add that they also elude the theologians and the psychologists. However, with the passing years, I understand better how it came about that the Jewish people fell victim to a scientifically designed program of mass demoralization leading to genocide, a cat and mouse game played by the ruthless killers on a variegated, confused population which was led to feeling alternating vague hope and despair. What comes mainly into question for me regarding these epic events is nothing less than the validity of the age-old, traditional image of God, for if this image entails, as it does, an omniscient, omnipotent, omnipresent God, author of our historical drama, and a belief in Israel as his chosen people, one would also have to accept the conclusion that it was God's will, part of his divine plan that Hitler condemn six million Jews to scientific premeditated slaughter.

For the Christians, the Jewish sin has been their failure to acknowledge the divinity of Christ. The sin for the Jew, according to orthodox belief: they did not sufficiently live up to God's commandments as set forth in the Torah. Ultra-orthodox Jews have even referred to European Jews of that time as the most sinful generation. In both cases, they were punished throughout their exile by a just and angry God. They deserved to suffer. Like Sartre, I am personally unwilling to carry an image of man as inescapably guilty before God or of suffering as inevitably merited–as divinely inflicted punishment for sin. Sartre wrote (2), that the alternative is to "end by praising and loving God for the indiscriminate annihilation of six million Jews".

Our past-holocaust God-image appears to be due for revision, for the brutality displayed was totally inconsistent with that of a wrathful, jealous, but also just Father-God who is ever-loving and forgiving; the God who chose his people, was chosen by them, and who promised never to abandon them. In his *Answer to Job* (3), Jung commented on the unfeeling, unconscious side of God (image) in crushing the innocent Job in order to appease his own inner doubts. Interpreted as one might a dream or myth, Job emerges morally superior to the cosmic megaforce called God who seeks out Job, his pious loyal servant, and appears to need the mirror of his reflecting consciousness in order to see Himself, to see His own dark side in reflection.

Perhaps a recognition that man was indeed created in God's image, one that embodies the potential of unfeeling destructiveness together with his loving-kindness and forgiveness would help us begin to comprehend the Nazi horror. "I form light and create darkness: I make peace and create evil..." says the unified God in Isaiah (xlv, 7). Christianity, by contrast, in resolving the question of the highly problematical God-image, relegated all the good to God and the evil to his rebellious son Satan, or onto the shoulders of mankind, a decisive split in Christian consciousness. We note here that man's ever changing image of God may be viewed, psychologically speaking, as a reflection of the changing level of awareness in mankind.

I do not believe that there can be any real peace of mind or heart for Jews everywhere until the fundamental questions raised above are earnestly confronted and responded to. I can live in respect and awe with a metaphysical God whose ways are inscrutable and beyond our comprehension. It is not for man to question the ways of god. However, this concept of God is not compatible with the traditional view of a God concerned with the welfare of his people: that he rewards obedience and punishes sin (disobedience). This statement does not, of course, eliminate the possibility of a teleological thrust, of goal-directedness in the metaphysical God concept.

By way of defense or explanation of God's role in the holocaust, many have maintained with some justification that the founding of the state of Israel would not have been possible but for that gruesome catastrophe. But what a price to pay for this longed for historical event! And who can be certain that another holocaust may not be in the making in view of the Arab hostility that unceasingly envelopes this fledgling state.

We too easily forget that the practical Zionism that led to the founding of the modern state of Israel was of a revolutionary nature, a frontal assault on the eighteen hundred year old ethos of the dispersed Jewish people. The ultra-orthodox of both the diaspora and of Israel still to this day do not recognize the state of Israel because its founding was not accompanied by the coming of the Messiah. It is still an open question whether Israel, with its prophetic, historic claim to be the place for the ingathering of the Jewish people can, in the long run, maintain its territory in the face of insufficient immigration. It has been stated on good authority that an additional one hundred thousand Jews present at the founding of the state would have altered its subsequent history in a most positive way.

In the entire history of the diaspora beginning with Babylon, no amount of admonition about the inevitability of anti-Semitic action or of the Jewish people's collective obligation to itself, its destiny, or its God has ever moved "free" Jewish masses to aliya. It is not likely to, now. Like other revolutionary movements of the 20th century, the problem of how the founding fathers and mothers can transmit their revolutionary zeal to the succeeding generations remains a timely one. Perhaps to be normal like other nations is not such a bad idea, though it does violence to the traditional self-image of being chosen-for whatever purpose–and of special interest to God, a priestly people and a light unto the nations. After all, other "normal" nations are also concerned with improving their people's physical and spiritual quality of life.

Biblical scholarship which demonstrated the multiple authorship of the Pentateuch is considered heretical by the orthodox rabbinate. Are we to believe that the earth was created 5745 years ago? Evolutionary geological and other cosmogonic hypotheses of modern science are likewise taboo. The bulk of modern orthodox Jews do not hold to these doctrines. Nor do they take literally the contention that God appeared to Moses on Sinai, spoke to him face to face and conveyed to him word for unalterable word his eternal laws to which Israel was bound forever, even in unfaithfulness. On the other hand, to perceive this divinely inspired doctrine as having been transmitted by gifted, prophetic individuals over a period of time, to be understood in symbolic and allegoric terms in entirely credible tome and to contemporary sensibility; more comprehensible to the modern Jew–with or without soul. It does not do violence to his rational intellect, an important component which also demands its due. The naive, anthropomorphic beliefs of our bronze-age ancestors and beyond undoubtedly served a centripetal unifying function. For many today they still do. But they can no longer be taken literally by the mass of modern Jews.

The bible is no less great or less inspiring for having been comprised by many Jewish hands, a composite work, a collection of sources and documents of various periods of time. Religions grow and change in major respects, the result of selection which is not considered arbitrary only by those who, as Zwi Werblowski stated it (4) "maintain that the one true religion (i.e. the one that the writer happens to subscribe to) sprang ready made from God as Pallus from Zeus". "But this view", he continues, "is no longer held by any reputable theologian, let alone by critical scholars." The heresy charge by the orthodox faithful is not taken seriously by orthodox Jews with liberal leanings.

I am well aware that the true essence of Judaism lies only partially with its liturgy or religious law. Equally important are the accompanying hopes of the people together with its customs, morals and rituals. These elements exist in a fluid state sustained by traditional acceptance. I personally live with two God-images, one a galactic "big-bang" power; a force-field creator that shapes our phenomenal reality. This God is an entity beyond our comprehension, an unknown and unknowable entity. The other is closer to human comprehension, a God whose imprint is in me. I have observed that when events become turbulent in my own life, when unsettling situations arise...when, as the saying goes, the water reaches the buttocks, I find myself with suspended critical faculties silently addressing the entity within myself, the image or imprint of God in me called the Self (as distinct from ego). This God-image or symbol assumes for me a more personal dimension which can be addressed in a human way. At such moments the cosmic megaforce power will not suffice. He or it is simply too remote, too far removed from my human need for more personal encounter and dialogue.

The metaphysical God-entity does not cease to exist or function for me at such times but is rather displaced for the occasion by a more paternal God-image better able to listen and respond sympathetically. Both of these God concepts are know to Jewish theology. The cosmic creator God is best described in the Kabbalah, in Jewish mysticism. I find myself in conflict here. I am aware of the strong centrifugal, assimilationist forces at work in the diaspora and would not like to visualize a world deprived of Judaism and what it represents one or five hundred years from now. I ask myself whether certain specific changes in Judaic traditional thinking may not serve to hold-together the disparate beliefs of world Jewry without violating the basic essence of Judaism. This is a remote hope because orthodox Jews generally regard both bible and talmud as God-given and unalterable except through the cumulative weight of rabbinic opinion over extended periods of time. In support of this viewpoint, it must be stated that this fundamental adherence served to keep Judaism alive through the centuries of exile and dispersion, a phenomenon unlike any other in history.

Among the many controversial issues that modern Jews in search of a soul contend with, a prime example is the "who is a Jew" problem that recurrently threatens government unity in Israel and stirs up a hornet's nest in the diaspora. Politically, the Israeli electoral system allows numerically tiny ultra-orthodox groups of Knesset members supported at times by modern orthodox members to challenge the stability of government by threatening to withdraw support on crucial issues. They can thereby attempt to gain their ends by a not-too-subtle form of blackmail. Their ends: a) increased financial support for yeshivot, their private religious schools and b) a state run in accord with halacha–Jewish religious law.

A Jew, defined by the "law of return" is one born of a Jewish mother or one converted to Judaism. Orthodox groups in the Knesset want the law to read...conversion "according to halacha". Practically speaking, such a change in the law would affect an insignificant number of immigrants. It would, however, effectively eliminate all possibilities of establishing religious pluralism in Israel. Conservative and reform rabbis are currently barred from performing all important religious rituals. The proposed law would insure a state-enforced orthodox monopoly in Israel, a condition which in fact exists today. A remedy for this and comparable situations would be a complete separation of church and state. Those who wish to follow ancient traditional ways are free to do so. In a democracy, customs and practices cannot be legislated and binding without the consent of the governed. On the other hand, church and state are inseparable in the minds of the traditionally oriented Jews; another dilemma!

Intimately connected with the "who is a Jew" problem is the role of Jewish women in traditional Jewish practice. I ask myself how it came about that a religion as patriarchally oriented as Judaism so completely disregards the role of the male element in the sexual union and bases its continuity and descent upon Jewish motherhood alone. In orthodox communities, the Jewish woman is quite rightly honored as mother and homemaker. She may not, however, appear as a witness in religious court proceedings. Unlike her counterpart in reform and most conservative circles, she is barred from serious talmudic studies and from aspiring to the post of the rabbinate. Genetic and inherited factors play no part in Jewish identity. But how can transmission of Jewish continuity be exclusively matrilinear if cultural, religious, and traditional historic elements are the real determinants of Jewish identity?

Matrilinear descent, currently being challenged and altered by reform movement of Judaism, is a fact of Jewish life that stems from third century rabbinic interpretation rather than from biblical sources. We should recall in this regard that our biblical Hebrew ancestors lived among Canaanite and other agricultural pagan people. Not surprisingly, they frequently deviated from their monotheistic beliefs and practices. It appears from biblical texts that portions of the Hebrew population fell-in from time to time with the compelling "power of earth", "mystery of fertility" practices of the polytheistic neighbors. Ashtarot and Baalim related to the earth-bound great mother archetype endemic to the regional agricultural societies about them became objects of worship. Biblical prophets repeatedly warned of catastrophe threatened by the jealous Yahweh in response to their "whoring after strange gods" rather than adhering to the one God.

The Yahwistic religion that emerged during their forty year long peregrination toward the promised land when released from Egyptian slavery could be seen as a sworn enemy, an antidote to the prevailing matriarchal nature religions of the region. Jungians are inclined to equate the appearance of this predominantly masculine God-image with a break-through in human consciousness out of the less differentiated, instinct-dominated matriarchal unconscious, matriarchal in that it gave birth to ego consciousness.

Rivkah Schaerf-Kluger, writing on the subject of the chosen people (5) states, "this masculine dominated religion represents the ascent of consciousness from the matriarchal primal womb of the natural religions. In this matriarchal religion", she continues, "women would even necessarily must, become the symbol of sinful libido, detached from Yahweh. The spiritual God Yahweh had struggled out of the maternal matrix of nature, the primal ground of pagan nature religions. Therefore the feminine was necessarily suppressed but was manifested in God's character, unconscious and negative." This discrimination is still evident today in the separation of men and women in orthodox synagogues and at the Western (wailing) wall in Jerusalem. Still today, ultra-orthodox men avoid public contact with women–to my mind a primitive defense against the numinous and the unclean.

Still on the subject of matrilinear descent, I personally favor the doctrine of reform Judaism that either parent may transmit Jewish identity. Such a change in orthodox law and custom would, I believe help considerably in countering the assimilationist tendency so evident in the diaspora today. On the other hand, it is maintained by the orthodoxy that at least one knows who the mother is. Paternity is open to question. I fail to see what essential difference this would make since genetic factors play no part in the drama. On the other hand, it is held–with justification–that changing the matrilinear custom could be highly divisive to world Jewry in that it would create for the orthodox, two marriage classes, the allowed and the forbidden. Such grouping would determine for the orthodox the marriage "moiety" out of which marriage is permissible, a disruption of the Jewish people at a time when unity is sorely needed. The issue is far from settled and the arguments go on, pro and contra.

I would not like to return to the question raised earlier; what is there about the Jew, about his God-image and relationship, and consequently his way of life that has so consistently evoked anti-Semitic responses from his host countries throughout his history culminating with the holocaust in our time. Anti-Semitism predated the Christian era. And surely the predator bears a large burden of responsibility for its creation. But the Jewish beliefs and way of life may not be left out of the equation. We know that minority groups within a host country everywhere are subject to suspicion, discrimination, and outright aggression. The Jew, however has been an especially sought out target throughout his history. Voltaire's *Dictionaire Philosophique* carries an item–the most extensive of the volume entitled "Jew–our master and enemies whom we detest... the most abominable people in the world". Prager and Telushkin (6) in their book on anti-Semitism demonstrate that while there is no single or simple explanation for anti-Semitism, one factor–that of chosenness–stands out prominently. To enlarge on the subject, generally, it is often mentioned that Jews are said to enjoy a certain degree of material well-being relative to their neighbors. We take note that Mosaic law made charity a religious obligation and Jewish poverty was less visible. Also interestingly is the fact that Eastern Jews who were poorest suffered the most. In North America, where they were most affluent, they suffered the least. Of interest too is that alcoholism was almost unknown and adherence to family life, a religious duty.

Christians whose religious doctrines contributed so much to Jewish persecution in the past are presently crucial allies and friends. Ghastly and obscene as the blood libel was in the past, its modern promulgators are to be found in the Moslem souks and in the Soviets, not in the churches. I concur with the authors of the book that a goodly part of the root of anti-Semitism is to be sought not in racism, xenophobia, economic factors, scapegoating, or in any other universalizing element, important as they are. It is thought by many that one of the prominent instigating factors for the hatred of the Jews is to be sought in one of the basic premises of Judaism itself.

It was generally understood and accepted by pre-modern Jews that their challenging religion was the main reason for their suffering. The religion itself has moulded the nationalism of the Jew, most strikingly demonstrated in what may be called probably the most provocative doctrine in history–that of chosenness. The claim that the Jews were chosen only for obligation and suffering is disingenuous. The danger of psychological inflation in such a doctrine is self-evident regardless of how it is understood or explained. It opens the way to a sense of election, of specialness and holiness, and for the non-Jewish world, to envy and mistrust.

I am well aware that I am treading on shaky grounds in this argument, for, say the orthodox, the doctrine of chosenness is so intrinsic a part of Jewish history and religion that an alteration of it would be destructive to its very essence. Though seemingly incomprehensible, this would amount to a "loss of soul", for the doctrine of chosenness belongs to the main storehouse of fundamental religious experience of the bible. So say the faithful. Possibly a psychological or symbolic understanding of this burdensome concept could restore its dignity by relating it, psychologically, to enhancement of human consciousness, the Jewish people being the ones chosen to carry this burden. In any case, Israel's choseness has been regarded as an irritating doctrine, offensive to other people, and modern Jews have felt themselves weighed down by it, longing for normalcy...to be like other people. "Jews", remarked Father Marcel DuBois whimsically, "are just like other people, only more so". Father DuBois, a Catholic priest is head of medieval philosophy at the Hebrew University in Jerusalem. Weary of being chosen, many Jews say, with Tevya, in effect, next time, please, choose someone else.

I am sadly aware of the limited scope and fragmentary nature of my comments and I am left with many ambivalences and unanswered questions which continue on in me together with the challenges for change. Orthodox sources ask, "How can Jews give up their time hallowed, God-given beliefs and practices and yet remain Jews?" They add, in effect, it's a tough club to belong to. Join it or leave it. In my discussion above, I have targeted the orthodox establishment. In order to do justice to it, I should mention that world orthodoxy is not a monolithic body. We may well ask when in the long history of Judaism was it ever single or unified?

In Israel, two divergent trends are evident, particularly as they related to Jewish nationalism: one is political nationalism, the other political restraint. The former believe we are in the era of Messianic redemption with a mystical perception that possession of the land, visualized within varying borders, is a divinely ordained inheritance. With zealous ecstasy and passion, their faith leads them to a total, a less than democratic, all embracing sacredness of reality. God inspired and God ordained. The other group is prepared to be more flexible and compromising in matters pertaining to land, Arab neighbors, and the holiness of the state of Israel.

I believe that the emergence of the greater possibility of individual freedom of choice, conscience, and responsibility in modern times calls for a broadening of outlook in Judaic thought. I also know that strongly held collective values and the notion of individual choice do not harmonize readily. On Yom Kippur, for instance, Jews ask forgiveness not as individuals but predominantly as a people. Have I in this paper, been more critical that I actually feel? Jews are the most self-critical people on earth. I do not think I diminish Judaism by calling into question some of the more controversial aspects of Jewish religious premises as they pertain to our current condition. On the contrary, an honest re-evaluation in depth could bring fresh interest and enthusiasm into our religious life.

As a psychologist, I understand that ego by itself is no match for this world. However, ego sustained by a relationship to a much larger, inner center in each of us, conceivably is. This larger center the Self, mentioned previously, is the hypothetical core of all psychic functioning. For me it serves as a bridge to the metaphysical God "out there", a symbol of wholeness, of totality. It also allows a perception of a more humanly personal God-image. Both images coexist and need not interfere with each other. Psychological experience steps in for me where pure faith falls short, a way into and through irreconcilable dilemmas. The soul lives "out there", but also within me, in each of us. Conceivably, a symbolic in-depth understanding of the problems involved is a way, possibly the way, for the modern Jew in search of soul.

REFERENCES

1. Rubenstein, R.L., *After Auschwitz*. (1976) Indianapolis, Bobbs-Merrill C.
2. Satre, Jean Paul, *The Anti-Semite And The Jew*. (1965) New York, Schocken Books.
3. Jung, C.G., *Answer to Job*. Collected Works, Vol. 11. (1958) Pantheon Book, New York.
4. Werblowski, Swi, Judaism or the Religion of Israel. In *The Concise Encyclopedia of Living Faiths*. (1962). Ed: E. Zahner. Beacon Press, Boston.
5. Kluger, R.S. *Psyche And Bible*. (1974) Spring Publications, Zurich.
6. Prager and Telushkin, *Why The Jews? The Reason For Anti-Semitism*. (1985) Simon and Schuster, N.Y.

Reflections at Age Eighty-Four
James Kirsch, M.D.

After a good deal of hesitation and much heart searching, I have decided to write my contribution to this book as a kind of autobiography. I am fully aware of the fact that any attempt to write anything about one's own history and development meets many obstacles. Hindsight is a special lens through which one sees certain events and distorts others in a special configuration. I will try to describe inner events as I remember them today.

I am also aware of the deceptive character of our memory, especially in regard to matters that are of great emotional importance to us. One of those images that stands out in my memory and would be classified by Freud's term of "Cover memory" (Deckerinnergung) was my firm conviction of many years that my father took me for many Sundays of the year to a bullfight in Guatemala, where I was born and spent the first six-and-a-half years of my life. It was only much later, while visiting my mother in Guatemala, I found out that there never was an arena for bullfights there, that these bullfights were a figment of my imagination. However much this memory proved to be an illusion in regard to facts, it turned out to be an important phantasy since it demonstrated the truly fatherly relationship my father had to me and what deep conflicts of collective character were symbolized by bullfights.

Another memory, however, from approximately the same period of my life in Guatemala, was a reference to the moon. We celebrate the Seder in the house. My father took me outside into the night, pointed at the moon and said: "On Seder evening there is always a full moon." Though both my parents loved me very much, it was my father who influenced my spiritual life greatly and decisively.

In 1980, a British company began to construct the first railroad in Guatemala. It ran from the capital to the main harbor on the Caribbean, Puerto Barrios. Standing at the pier of the embarkation, I fell into the relatively deep and dirty water and was drowning when somebody fished me out of the water as I came up for the third time. I was completely passive in the water, I remember, and all the events of my short life (I was six-and-a-half years old) passed before my eyes. It was a wonderful show; scenes that started from sometime after my birth came in strictly historical order. Thus, they demonstrated to me the power and numinosity of what later I would call by the scientific name "the unconscious."

Writing one's autobiography always means that one is selective in the choice of memories. One tells pleasant, meaningful memories and suppresses anything unpleasant. In the case of this book, one is even asked to be selective. I choose some of the events in which an invasion of the unconsciousness took place. It is autobiographical only in the sense that I speak about inner events which indicated to me that I am Jewish, though not in the sense in which my orthodox family considered itself Jewish. These events might explain why I felt so strongly that I am Jewish but cannot join any synagogue nor identify with a Jewish social group.

Later, when I lived with my family in Breslau, the capitol of the German province, Silesia (now a Polish city), I was very much impressed by a few of my dreams. Since I had private Hebrew lessons and studied the Hebrew Bible, I read the story of Joseph with great interest. He had dreams and interpreted them. So I paid attention to my dreams and tried to interpret them; I also drew conclusions from them. I still remember two of these dreams quite vividly from sometime in 1909. In the first, I saw a tremendous locomotive, of a size I had never seen in real life, cross the border of Silesia into Germany from the east. At that time, I took dreams literally. This dream meant to me that Russia would soon invade Germany. The other dream had immediate practical consequences for me. I dreamt that the seven dwarves of the Snow White fairy tale were carrying a casket made of glass, underground. In it was Snow White. What I was seeing was her subterranean funeral, but I also knew that she was not really dead. I was quite shocked and awoke with a thumping heart. I thought immediately that little Snow White was really my brother who as three yeas younger than myself. We had many fights at that time. However, after this dream, I felt very guilty and decided never to attack him again. In fact, I never fought with him again. My mother never understood why there was suddenly peace between her sons. Throughout my life, I frequently thought and meditated on this childhood dream and had, of course, quite a different interpretation. Today, I know that Snow White represented my "anima" and that it was my task to bring her back to life. I believe that in my life this apparently dead soul has come back to life.

In 1910, my family moved to Berlin. Again, I had Hebrew lessons, this time from a young orthodox Jew whom I liked very much. It was he who was preparing me for my Bar Mitzvah, which was to take place on the Sabbath of the 8th of August, 1914. I was with my family in Travemunde, a seaside resort on the Baltic Sea, for the greater part of July. During the last week of July 1, I was bothering my mother every day with telling her that the Russians had mobilized 10 army corps and were threatening to invade Germany. I urged her to let us go home, to return to Berlin immediately. My mother finally gave in and took the train on July 30th, just in time to avoid the German mobilization, which made travelling by civilians impossible for several weeks. My family, fortunately, was not gripped by the enthusiasm and fervor with which the European nations greeted the outbreak of the war. It was only sometime after the war that I found out that the Russians had actually mobilized 10 army corps many weeks before August 1st, 1914. My unconscious knew what was coming and certainly was most disturbed by all the developments that led to the war.

It was also during the last week of July 1914, when the human psyche was in a great upheaval, that a most important event happened in my life, an event which I never mentioned to my friends or to my analysts. It just never came up in my analytical interviews until I decided one day to tell the details of this event to Jung. Now, I want to relate it to my readers in the hope that they will appreciate what such an invasion of the unconsciousness meant to a boy of 13. Even now, I have to overcome a great deal of resistance, but I feel I must tell it because it is important for the understanding of myself and the course my life took. It might be of help to somebody who at critical times in his life might be overtaken by a numinous experience.

It happened in Travemunde on one of the mornings of the last week in July of 1914. It was beautiful weather. I was walking alone through a little wood. I was not thinking of anything in particular when I suddenly heard a voice speaking very clearly in me: "You shall become like Abraham and Moses and found a new people." I was dumbfounded, and for weeks I did not know what to make of it. At that time, it was extremely unclear to me what the message in particular meant. Otherwise, my life continued to run in a very ordinary way. I went to school; I was a good student. Besides, I received religious education, as most Jewish teenage boys received in those days in Germany. But I kept my secret. The went on far from Berlin. I was the only Jew in the upper classes of my high school. I had collisions of anti-Semitism with my school pals. I joined the "Blau-Weiss," a Zionistic hiking youth club through which I came in touch with many Jewish boys and a few Jewish girls. With some of them, who later emigrated to Israel, I remained friends until their deaths.

One of the effects of my experience was that, after meditation on it every day for a whole year, I decided, at the age of 14, to give up all dietary laws, believing that I did not need to keep any of these laws since I had a direct connection with God.

Under the influence of the Zionist hiking club, the "Blau-Weiss," I became quite Zionistic myself. From some of these friends, I found out what the real situation of the German war machine was. My father was in Guatemala. Naturally, we had no communication with him during the war. My mother avoided any kind of support of the German army. So, as a compromise, I joined the "Hiflsdienst" (auxiliary service) after finishing school at the early age of 17.

My "work" consisted of carrying empty French and English gas grenades from one room of the Museum of Gas Shells to another room, then back again to the first room. On the 9th of November, 1918, I heard in the morning that an armistice had been declared on the Western front. The war was over. This was the end of my "hilfsdienst." I simply walked out of the "Museum," never to return. While I was standing in the street, waiting for a street car, I suddenly heard, again, a low voice speaking to me. This time it said: "There is a man who should have been killed in the war but was not. He will try to kill the Jews." In my opinion, God had spoken to me again. I took this statement of the "voice" very seriously. I never doubted that it told me the truth and that is message was a genuine prophecy. While I was studying Medicine, my soul was attentive to everything that was going on in Germany and the world. I tried to identify the man whom the warning voice had characterized as Killer of the Jews. When the first "Hitlerputsch" occurred in 1921, I knew at once he was the man whom the warning voice had referred to. Throughout the 20s and the beginning of the 30s, I knew what fate was waiting for us Jews. I warned many of my Jewish friends, but mostly to no avail.

Well-prepared by the voice, I knew what to do when Hitler was elected chancellor. This historical event occurred on January 30th, 1933. On the 31st, I went to the police station and got passports for myself and my whole family. I had a wide and a daughter, and another child was on the way. I was married in 1926, and by 1933, I had a flourishing practice as a Jungian analyst. I left Berlin in August 1933, went to Palestine, and the, for no conscious reason, I began to teach myself English. I had no idea that in the course of my life I would live in English-speaking countries only and that English would become the language of all my thoughts and feelings.

In 1928, I had met Jung personally at the Congress of the International Society for Psychotherapy in Baden, Germany. There were no photographs of him around. When I came into the lobby of the hotel, there were many men, probably psychologists and psychiatrists, sitting in big comfortable chairs; I went straight up, like an arrow shot from a bow, to one man and said–in German of course–Dr. Jung. I am James Kirsch." He got up from his chair and said, "Glad to know you. Are you an American? I was astonished and stumbled with my answer, "Yes–oh, no!" Then I explained that I was born in Guatemala and had spent some time in New York, as a boy. Then I asked him, How did you know? He replied, "By the way you moved your ankles."

The following year, 1929, I started my analysis with him. One of my first dreams was: A voice said: "There is relative evil and there is absolute evil." Jung became quite moved, got up from his chair, and we discussed this apodictic statement of the unconscious for quite some time. Little did I know at that time that absolute evil would soon break out. At that time, Jung gave a seminar in which he discussed the dreams of an American woman. Somehow, the events which Jung saw outlined in some of her visions reminded me of my anticipation of Hitler. Watching my own dreams and remembering the voice that spoke to me on the 9th of November, 1918, I was confirmed in my conviction, on hearing his seminar, that I would have to leave Germany soon.

I knew the greatness of Jung from the time, in 1922, when I first read *Psychological Types*. In reading the chapter on Prometheus and Epimetheus, I suddenly realized that Jung "had been there." By that, I meant that he had entered the divine realm and had received uncommon knowledge from God, Himself. I always remained his friend and frankly and unreservedly accepted his guidance, his interpretation of dreams, his understanding of the nature of the unconscious. However, we differed very sharply in 1933, when he had forgotten his understanding of the German unconscious as he had described it in a paper written in 1918. I did not accept his advice that I stay on in Germany, even though he said that the Nazi system would be over in six months. When I saw him for the first time years later, in 1947, after the Second World War, the first words he spoke to me were those of sincere apology for the advice he had given me in 1933. "Of course you were right, not I," he said.

It was at the time that I left Germany that the question of whether we Jews were a nation or a religion moved me very much. As a Zionist, I decided we were a nation. But, then, I could not reconcile this notion with the fact that practically all our customs, festivals, and traditions were in direct connection with a religious event or tradition. If we Jews were a nation, then it would be all right to belong to any religion, for example, to any of the hundreds of Protestant denominations. But this was obviously not the case. If a Jew converted to another religion, he was considered by Jews to be a loss to the Jewish people. Only Hitler's brand of anti-Semitism regarded a race as the decisive factor in determining who was Jewish. It was only after studying comparative religions and especially those of so-called "primitive" societies, (Primitive: in the sense of not belonging to any of the world religions, like Christianity, Buddhism, Islam, etc.), that I understood that, for them, culture, tradition, art and religion were one thing–all of one texture–like that of the Navajos. These cultures did not rest so much on a belief system but rather on rituals, customs and festivals that were practiced by all members of the tribe and represented a collective connection with the collective unconscious. In the same sense, we Jews held on to common customs, rituals and traditions throughout biblical times and those of the exile, based on certain fundamental and slowly-changing attitudes to the collective unconscious. It as important for me to find out what was the common denominator in Jewish history. At long last, I found an answer that satisfied me to a high degree. It was that Jewish history represented a process of *individuation*, lasting several thousand years.

It began with the statement in the creation story (Genesis I) that "God divided the light from the darkness," that "God made the firmament from the waters which were above the firmament." In psychological terms, a division took place in the collective unconscious, a fact that created tension in the human psyche and forced man to become conscious. Furthermore, God said, (Genesis I:26), "Let us make man in our own image, in the image of God created He him, male and female created He them." These verses in the very first chapter of the Holy Scripture represented the beginning of man becoming conscious and the necessity of man to fulfill the image of God in himself.

I understand the history of the Jewish people, their prophets, mystics, cabbalists, "false" Messiah figures and the hasidim as progressive and regressive steps in the development of consciousness. In the course of Jewish and world history, I was placed at the stage where God revealed Himself psychologically. The experiences I had at the time before my Bar Mitsvah and the one on the day of the armistice in 1918 were such steps and had to be seen as a tiny part of the continuing revelation of God in man–or to say the same thing modern scientific language–as continuing information which comes from the unconscious into the conscious. They have to be understood as psychological messages to me as an individual. The first, at the age of 13, was definitely a personal message which, only in its consequences, had a somewhat wider meaning. It included my sons and many other people whom I introduced into Jungian psychology.

Considering the effects which the process of individuation had on my own personality, I realized it imposed on me a further problem for which I have not yet found a satisfactory answer. The fact that the uninterrupted process of individuation, on one side, has brought greater consciousness to myself, on the other hand, also taught me how other human beings of different nationalities relate to their traditions and to the collective unconscious. In other words, I learned to appreciate the viewpoints and backgrounds of other people. I experienced what I had in common with them and where I was different. I was not a physician for Jews alone but for people of other backgrounds, as well. While in other generations, our prophets, let's say, or the cabbalists, always directed their messages to the Jews only, my knowledge–my contact with the collective unconscious–goes to anyone who wants my knowledge because I am not limited to the parochial attitude of many Jews but am open to the universal message of the great prophets. As a psychologist, I have been in contact with many Christians of different denominations as, also, with Taoists, Muslims and others.

Where is, then, the future of the Jewish people? Since contact with the collective unconscious means a widening and deepening of individual consciousness and relationship to all kinds of human beings, is there room and necessity for the existence of a special group? Would the national ego of the Jewish people have a "raison d'etre" for continued existence? What is the inner reason why, in spite of all the persecutions and slaughter of our people, we Jews have been kept alive for almost 4000 years? We are still here. Is our historical task fulfilled? Would the new understanding which modern psychology brought to Western culture support or invalidate the future existence of the Jews?

It certainly must end the parochial and nationalistic behavior of many Jews and Jewish groups for whom to be Jewish is simply an enlargement of the ego. Or will the universal image of God, as it is expressed by several of the Old Testament prophets, allow the Jews to continue to exist as an enlightened community with the rest of mankind?

With my training as a physician and a psychiatrist, along with my analysis with Jung, I became a Jungian analyst, a psychiatrist, a psychologist who was willing to help all kinds of human beings, irrespective of race, color, sex–or religion. In understood that religion had a great deal to do with psychology, but I did not know what the connection between the two was. For a long time, these two were like two wheels revolving around two different centers in my soul until it finally dawned on me that the two were really one, that there is such a thing as the collective unconscious, a deeper layer in the psyche, a source of infinite knowledge, containing definite patterns of behavior which Jung called "archetypes." I realized that the "voice" had come from the collective unconscious. Deeply moved by the declaration of the armistice and the total defeat of Germany, the collective unconscious (Jung's term for the deepest layer of the human psyche) was charged with numinosity and had sent a message about the future.

In the course of time, I learned more and more about the collective unconscious and the archetypes–structures which came to consciousness in different ages, on different levels, in different projections onto heaven, earth, stones, or people and, thus, determined the special character of cultures. As much as possible, I, as a physician, should be open to all the varieties in which human beings relate to these archetypes and express them. My function as physician of the soul as to help men and women related to these archetypes, to make man and his society whole, as healthy as possible.

In this effort–which is, of course, not always successful–I am assisted by all the utterances of the unconscious, itself, be they dreams, visions, or auditory experiences. If the "patient" is willing and able to receive, he can become whole.

I am no more subject to sudden invasions by the unconscious, but the channel to and from the unconscious is not steadily open. I accept every hint the unconscious gives me in the form of dreams, visions, or auditory phenomena.

Looking back at the experience I had at the age of 13, shortly after my birthday but before my Bar-mitzvah, I can see how these words, "You will be like Abraham and Moses," fulfilled themselves. What I had in common with these ancestors was that I had visions like these two men had. One became the father of two peoples, through his sons Isaac and Ishamel; the other became the visionary, the liberator and law-giver of the Jewish people. My life naturally went through similar experiences and fulfillments, though on a much smaller scale, since I am living in the 20th century and life presented me with different tasks. Two of my sons became Jungian analysts, my daughter a psychiatric social worker. On the other hand, through me, many people became Jungian analysts or deeply involved in Jungian psychology. Though I have not started a new law, I helped many people to develop psychologically.

I realize that I have not responded exactly to the title of this book: rather, I have describe how I, as a young Jew of 13 and 17 found the soul. Through the tortuous ways of life, I found my way from these early experiences to the deep and comprehensive understanding of the unconscious that C.G. Jung achieved. But that is a different chapter with a different title.

Part Three

REFLECTIONS AND MANIFESTATIONS:
Life Variations to Soul

"The question I put before you, as well as before myself, is the question of the meaning of Judaism for Jews.

Why do we call ourselves Jews? Because we are Jews? What does that mean: we are Jews? I want to speak to you not of an abstraction but of your own life, of our own life; and not of our life's outer hustle and bustle, but of its authenticity and essence."
–Martin Buber, *On Judaism*

Illustration by Martin Mondrus

Marvin's Grandfather - oil painting 1943.
I was fascinated by this impressive gentleman. He represented the authentic Jewish religious identity to me. He was like the Jew who survived intact through the centuries, with all the visual beauty and religious warmth.

Jewish Pictures
Martin Mondrus

I selected these particular works for their Jewish qualities–I could have added many others–although I was not consciously searching for such themes at the time. One could say that I was portraying my own life experiences in all my work and, as a Jew, that was bound to be part of it. Some of these, such as "Moses," are more symbolic in their themes, whereas others, such as "My Father's Truck" are quite personal. Still others, such as "Marvin's Grandfather" and "My Mother and Father in the Kitchen," are both personal and, I hope universal.

My Mother and Father in the Kitchen - wash drawing 1943.
This was a familiar scene for me. My parents were early risers and often sat despondent, laden with worries: financial and otherwise.

My Father's Truck - watercolor 1944.
The various trucks my father had during his years as a junk collector loomed with major importance in our family life. His work, precarious as it was, was the sustenance of the family. It also symbolized his station in life. He was honest, hard-working, humble in some areas, but proud and strong in his Jewish consciousness. On weekends, his truck was often used for helping in major personal interests, Jewish education, and anything connected with the Workmen's Circle Organization.

Moses - oil painting 1952.
This painting, done in my twenty-seventh year, was my visualization of Moses as a humble but heroic figure, strong yet burdened with concern for the fate of his people, symbolized by the Jerusalem-like city in the background. This painting was exhibited at the Pasadena Art Institute in 1952 and featured in the Los Angeles Times Art Section.

Adam's Quest - etching 1972.
The theme of Justice was given to a group of printmakers by the Westside Jewish Community Center in 1972. My choice of Adam's Quest developed after much thought and introspection. The figure apart is Adam, and the bird symbolizes man's eternal quest for justice.

Hasidic Dancers - etchings. Two figures 1973.
My interest in music and dance goes back as far as I can remember. Marvin and I did Russian dances at weddings and bar-mitzvahs and we ushered at ballets and concerts during our high school years. Hasidic dancing came almost via osmosis and always touched me as part of my heritage.

Drawing of My Mother - pen and ink, 1979.
This pen and ink drawing was done while we were waiting in the doctor's office for her to be seen by her physician. She had suffered a stroke and her eyes no longer seemed to synchronize. He hands now seemed limp, but were still graceful. They were one of her best features. This drawing was done about six or seven months before her death. I guess I knew at this time that she would not be my devoted model many more times.

I Remember Anna - etching, 1980.
This etching is a combination photo collage and aquatint. It was done as a personal commemoration and tribute to my Mother, in 1980, the year of her death. The work emphasizes her youth and background in Russia. The word Staradub, her shtetl, is printed in Russian and shown here on the back of one of the photographs. The old couple, seated side-by-side, are my Mother's parents. This is all that I knew of them, since they died in Russia before I was born. People say that I look like my grandfather. I feel deprived that I never knew them.

Portrait of my Father - oil on canvas, 1943.

My father was always one of my favorite models. His strong facial features and hands appealed to me and mirrored his natural identification as a working man. He enjoyed posing as much as I did painting him and was proud that this son was an artist. We worked together all of one day to produce this work. I had just turned eighteen and was preparing for my first one-man exhibit.

Portrait of Leah, Marvin's Grandmother - oil on canvas, 1946.
I did this painting shortly after the war and my discharge from the Merchant Marine. It was meant to be a companion piece to the earlier one of her husband, Jacob, in 1943. She was some fifteen to twenty years his junior, but was well into her seventies at this time. (She died in her nineties!). Her warmth, earthiness and humor appealed to me very much and the "dress with red top" that she wore was especially stimulating. The obvious influence of van Gogh's "La Berceuse" was intentional, since the artist had a great impact upon me in my youth.

Street Scene - pen and ink drawing, 1942.
The old man walking in this drawing made his presence known in many of my works of this period. He was an example of many of the beloved old Jews I saw in my neighborhood of West Adams and Pico in my adolescent days.

Portrait of Rabbi Jacob Sonderling - charcoal drawing, 1953.
This drawing was from memory, several days after the wedding of Marvin Spiegelman and Ryma. Rabbi Sonderling officiated and I was best man at this moving ceremony. I looked at the Rabbi's face very intently while he spoke his lovely words in Hebrew and English. Here was a face where gentleness and beauty were competing with wisdom and experience. I wish that I could have arranged for Rabbi Sonderling to have posed for me. My memory sketch seems to have captured some of the qualities that, in turn, touched me.

Out of the Ashes - etching, 1973.
This etching was made for a travelling print-show sponsored by the Westside Jewish Community Center of Los Angeles to commemorate the 25th anniversary of Israel. Participating artists were given the theme of Hatikvah, or "Hope." My etching portrays the tragedy of the Holocaust in the lower circle and the prophetic fulfillment of the return to the Jewish homeland in the upper one.

Self-Portrait with a Rabbi - oil painting on canvas, 1983.
I painted this work after a painful encounter involving my heritage. In this painting, I am standing and holding my brushes–indicating who I am, what I do, and what is the central meaning of my life. The Rabbi suggests my connection with my Jewish heritage. I may not have been a traditional member of a congregation, but nevertheless, there is no doubt about my roots and their importance in my life.

Hasidic Dancer - monotype, 1985.
This is the most recent of my many drawings, paintings and etchings of religious Jews. I have noted that most Jews enjoy or are attracted to the happy dancing figures, "fraylach," but fewer want to live with the more somber subjects.

J. Marvin Spiegelman's Comment on
ARTWORK BY MARTIN MONDRUS

Mondrus is too modest about his "Jewish theme" work here. When he and I met as boys at the Workmen's Circle Camp in the summer of 1939, he had already completed a mural there on the suffering that Jews are undergoing in Germany. And, over the years, he has done considerable work of this nature. Of the examples presented here, several are more intimate for me, too. "Marvin's Grandfather," of course, is the same person that I speak of in my own contribution to this book, the man who, for me, too, embodied the Jewish tradition. Martin's father's truck and his parents were also familiar to me: many were the joyful times we had as youths at his house. These paintings were completed and were part of Mondrus' first "one-man-show" when he was 18, in 1943, before going into the military service. The later works are all known to me, of course, and carry a kind of color quality which is also quite moving. The group of Hasidic dancers (which hangs in my office) is especially vibrant and always touches people when they see it. Mondrus has remarked that everyone like the joyous works but tend to flinch with others that portray more somber themes. It has been a privilege for me to share a friendship of forty-six years with a man of such depth and perception.

The Way of the Orthodox
Robert A. Rosen, M.D.

It is my privilege to be able to contribute to this book in the hope of helping lost Jewish souls find their way home. This is essentially a problem of the Diaspora, the Exile from our physical and spiritual home since the destruction of the Second Temple in 70 c.e., but it is especially true of this Post-Holocaust Generation. I believe that it may be fruitful to retrace some of my personal path in regard as an illustration.

My great, great grandfather, Avraham Yitzchak, of the tribe of Levi, was a physician in a small town in Russia. His son, my great grandfather, Yeruchim Yaakov, was a Torah scholar in the same town. His son, my grandfather, Menachem Mendel, studied Torah in the Yeshiva in the little town of Kravitz near Vilna. He came to the United States in 1913 leaving behind him several brothers and sisters as well as his mother. Some of these siblings escaped the Nazis when they invaded Russia-Poland. His mother was shot to death while sitting in her kitchen and hiding the other members of the family beneath the kitchen floor. Menachem Mendel moved to Chicago, started his own business and became partially assimilated into America. He did not believe that it was possible to maintain his Orthodoxy while attempting to function in a Christian society. Thus, his son, my father, Yisrael Labe, become even more assimilated. Menachem Mendel and Yisrael Labe wanted to have another physician in the family as there had not been one for several generations. My mother, Miriam Chaya, was the last child of Rivka and Daniel Friedman who had also become assimilated in Chicago. Daniel was the son of a Russian Rabbi, Chuna.

My mother had no special problem with the birth of my older sister, Taibe, but when she became pregnant again, she was advised by her physician to have an abortion because of danger to her health. She declined. When I was born, they named me Raphael (the name of the Angel of Healing) who is the primal physician. The name comes from two Hebrew words. Rofeh meaning to heal (or physician), and A-l which is one of the names of G-d which reflects the attribute of loving kindness. Thus the concept of healing through the attribute of the loving kindness of G-d.

My formal education in Judaism occurred at an Orthodox Temple through the direction of Menachem Mendel. However the practice on a daily basis at home was more Conservative-Reform. This lent considerable confusion to my development. Furthermore, I had another source of confusion in the standard Orthodox teaching itself. I found that there were two categories of questions that I could ask at school. One was a very good question to which my teachers knew the answer. They would rejoice over the brilliant questions I asked. The secondary category included questions which I thought were even more brilliant. However, the response I received to those was "Do not ask such questions". I thus found myself floundering in a schizoid situation, which after a number of years, caused me to fall away from this distortion of the Orthodox approach and seek a more assimilated foundation for my life.

I knew that there was great substance to the Jewish Religion and ultimate truth to its teachings. However, I could not understand the true essence of what these teachings were. I also saw little connection to how this related to my daily life. When I would learn tracts of Talmud, they might involve issues such as the law regarding who was responsible for the injury to a cow who stepped in a hole in a road. I was living in Chicago at that time, and the relevance of a cow seemed light years away. I thus left my Hebrew education and concentrated on my secular American education. I left Chicago and attended U.C.L.A. I did well in school, but also adopted American secular value systems. This led to neglect of the Holy Covenant, the Torah itself, and eventually to marriage with an assimilated Jewish woman. I went to medical school in San Francisco and became a physician. This, unfortunately, meant that I was knowledgeable in disorders of the body, but not in health of the body-mind-spirit.

I moved to Boston for my internship and residency in disease medicine, and became even more Reformed in my approach to religion. It seemed that my intellect could, and should, be the judge of what was "right" and what was "wrong". I decided which portions of the Torah were "relevant" to modern society and which were archaic holdovers from the Middle Ages. I disregarded inconvenient or difficult commandments as I did not consider them to be real or important. This is essentially the approach of Reform Judaism today.

Fortunately, even though I was not on the highest spiritual plane, my intentions were to have a son who would be of the highest order. And G-d, in his Mercy, overlooked my defects and blessed me with a very high level soul as my son. Aharon (the high priest of Israel), who was born at this time.

All seemed to be going well until the foundations of my belief system were shaken by my divorce. I went through a period of re-examining everything that I had assumed to be true, to see which of my beliefs were grounded in solid foundation and which were sitting on quicksand. I found that many of the things I had previously assumed to be true could not be substantiated either by literature or by experience, and that many of "my" ideas were clearly wrong! In fact, I began to see how I unknowingly played a part in the development of the divorce setting because of these invalid "corrections" which I inserted into the Torah!

I began investigating everything that would be presented before me to see if I could establish a new foundation of truth for myself. I moved back to California and started evaluating a number of different spiritual philosophies including Zen Buddhism. I found that many of their concepts appeared to be very solid. These included such things as: not focusing on materialism, working on one's spiritual essence, quieting the mind and focusing on the oneness of the universe. I was confused as to how the Zen Buddhist could know eternal truths separate from the religion of the one G-d. I still didn't know how to understand or incorporate the teachings of the Torah into my life.

During this period of awakening and confusion, another great event occurred. I was crossing a street at Fisherman's Wharf in San Francisco, in a cross walk, and was struck by a car that was speeding over one of the hills. The car was going over 30 mph and did not brake until after the impact. I sustained several significant injuries including concussion, lacerations, broken bones, and internal bleeding. However, the most significant impact was psycho-spiritual.

I was unconscious for a considerable period of time, and even now, several years later, I still have complete amnesia for the actual event. I remember walking in an area some blocks away from the scene and thinking about doing something which I believed at the time was perfectly acceptable. Yet, I now know that I would have been in serious violation of the Torah if the accident had not stopped me from proceeding.

The next thing I recall was waking up in the Emergency Room. The question than arose as to where "I" was during the interim. Where were my Nefesh, Ruach, and Neshamah (three subdivisions of a Jewish Soul)? Did I travel to the Next World and return? Did I spiritually and/or physically die?

The next dilemma was to understand how this could have happened to ME! How did I come to be just in the wrong place at the right time? And how did I survive such an impact (assuming that I did!)?

I was physically immobilized with casts, crutches, and weakness and thus had a lot of time to ponder these issues. I went through a period of being afraid to go to sleep for fear that my soul would leave and come back this time. I thought I might evolve past this if I could gain some control over the soul-body connection. I studied Robert Monroe's "Journeys Outside the Body" and did achieve some ability to produce an "out of body" experience. This demonstrated conclusively to my scientific mind that there is more to life than that which is tangible. Thus, it came to me that it may be true that the Torah *is* describing things to us which are beyond our understanding and imagination; "For as the Heavens are higher than the earth, so are My ways...and thoughts...higher than yours, says the L-rd" (Isaiah 55:8). And if this is true, then there is the possibility that there was a direct relationship between the spiritual effects of my actions and the physical events that were occurring in my life. And then the awesome possibility that *ALL* of the things which are stated in the Torah, including those I couldn't understand are *TRUE*!

I thus went and re-examined my previous Hebrew teachings with my new Zen and spiritual perspectives and had a startling experience. It had seemed previously as if Judaism was all form without substance, and then there were Zen and other spiritual phenomena which were all substance without form. When the two came back together it was like air rushing back into a vacuum; like water filling up an empty vessel; like positive and negative poles, or right and left brain, reuniting to make a complete oneness!

With this new energy charging my system I began to dive back into my previous Jewish studies so that I could reconnect these separated parts. I learned that when Moses received the Torah at Mt. Sinai, he was given two divisions of the law. One was the Written Law which I had previously seen and not been able to understand. The other was the Oral Law, which I had not previously known, which contained the answers to all of my questions and also answers to questions I hadn't even thought of! Its general ideas in many ways paralleled the Zen teachings. I was still unclear about this interaction until I began rereading the Bible in its entirety. I read in Genesis, Chapter 25, that Avraham had other children at the end of his life and that he did not want them to interfere with the inheritance of his primary son, Yizchak. "He then gave them gifts and sent them to live in the East." It seemed to me that this East meant Far East, and that the gifts were the spiritual gifts of partial understanding of the Torah. I have since learned from commentary on the Zohar, the Book of Splendor which is one of the main sources of mystical Kabbalistic understanding in our tradition, that this is indeed what occurred.

About this time, a colleague invited me to assist him in the delivery of health care in a small town (Duncan, Oklahoma). I decided to go for both professional and spiritual reasons. The Reformed environment in California seemed to be more of a detriment than an asset to my spiritual progress. The lack of a Jewish community in rural Oklahoma in a way could be helpful in providing me with a clear space to study and grow; something similar to the isolation in the desert that had been of value to some of our great masters.

I moved there and began a Holistic practice of medicine (caring for a person's health of body, mind, and spirit; prevention preferred to crisis care) as well as my intense study of Jewish teachings. As I began to read, I saw that there were statements which were eternally true, and that the Torah is not man-made, nor of this world at all! It is infinite. The stories that are described indeed physically happen but they represent the original forces of creation which a human would not be able to discern of his own. Thus we speak of the Torah as a gift from G-d which provides an explanation and guide for human which is beyond their own capacity for comprehension.

The truths in this book are beyond time and space. Examples would be the awesome phenomena of the 17th day of the Hebrew month of Tammuz and the 9th day of the Hebrew month of Av.

On the 17th of Tammuz, 2104 b.c.e., Noah sent out the first dove to search for land, but she came back without finding a place to rest. Metaphorically, this represents the inability of exiles Israel to find rest or a peaceful dwelling in the non Jewish world: "And among these nations shalt thou have no repose, and there shall be no rest for the sole of the foot." (Deut. 28:65). Then, on this date 1314 b.c.e., Moses broke the original tablets of the Ten Commandments, which had been made by G-d, when he saw the Golden Calf. In 586 b.c.e., the walls of Jerusalem were breached by the attacking Babylonians, and then again on the same day in 70 c.e., the attacking Romans also broke through the walls of the city! At that time, the temple sacrifices ceased due to lack of animals for offering. Also, in 55 c.e., an idol was placed in the Temple and the Romans burned a Torah scroll.

On the 9th of Av, in 1314 b.c.e., the spies which Moses had sent to scout the land of Canaan gave a fearful report, due to their lack of complete trust in G-d. On this basis, the former slaves were afraid to follow Moses, under G-d's protection, into the land. They thus had to spend 40 years of spiritual purification in the desert until they reached the level required to enter into the Holy Land. Also on this day in 586 b.c.e. the First Temple was destroyed by the Babylonians, and on the same day in 70 c.e. the Second Temple was destroyed by the Romans! More recently, the expulsion of all Jews from Spain occurred on this day in 1942 c.e.

The recurring dates for these tragedies are not a coincidence. Rather, this is a graphic demonstration, over centuries, of the intrinsic negative nature of the force fields of that cyclical period in time. This is then translated into human terms for us by the timeless Torah through the unfolding of history.

There are also numerous examples of Torah knowledge that have preceded scientific knowledge by thousands of years. In particular, I am most intrigued by the description of one of the earliest aspects of creation on a spiritual level which preceded the physical world. At that time, G-d created the primordial light which was contained in a spiritual vessel. This vessel then became weakened and shattered. The light then exploded out into space and we are still engaged in the process of regathering the Holy Sparks. More than 3000 years later a secular Jewish scientist (Albert Einstein) demonstrated that our physical universe started out as a central mass of star material (physical light) which then exploded (the Big Bang Theory) and caused the current dispersion of the stars and planets as we know them today. Is this a coincidence? Unlikely?

Another example of the timelessness of the Torah is the description 3,500 years ago of the course of modern Jewish history. Moses confirms to the Children of Israel that they have made a contract with G-d which is binding upon them and their descendants forever. We are to be a nation of Holy People and are not allowed to do things that the other nations (who do not have this obligation) may do. We are under a completely separate system of rules: "He tells His words of Torah to Yaakov, His statutes and ordinances to Yisrael. He has not done so for other nations, and they do not know His ordinances. Praise the L-rd." (Psalm 147).

If we follow these guidelines we will receive blessings (positive feedback) beyond those of ordinary human circumstance. This would include protection and elevation from the ordinary problems of life on this level of creation. As G-d tells Avraham in Genesis 22:18 "And all the nations of the earth shall bless themselves by your descendants, because you have obeyed my voice." And again as G-d told Moses in Numbers 15:37-41: "...make for yourselves fringes on the corners of your garments throughout your generations...and you shall look upon them and remember *All* the commandments of the L-rd and fulfill them, and you will not follow after your heart and after your eyes by which you go astray–so that you may...be Holy to your G-d", "so that your days...may be prolonged...as the *days of heaven on earth.*" (Deuteronomy 11:21).

But if we do not follow those rules we will receive curses (negative feedback) beyond those of ordinary human experience. Thus we would be left unprotected from the antagonistic forces of nature, the jealousy of the other nations, and the temptations of our own minds. Some excerpts from the section in Deuteronomy 28 which relate specifically to this bipolar issue are as follows:

> **And it shall come to pass, if thou shalt harken diligently unto the voice of the L-rd thy G-d, to observe to do all His commandments, that the L-rd will set thee on high above all the nations of the earth. And there shall come upon thee all these blessings, and overtake thee: Blessed shalt thou be in the city, and blessed shalt thou be in the field. Blessed shall be the fruit of thy body...thy land...thy cattle...and the basket. Blessed shalt thou be when thou come in...and when thou go out. The L-rd will cause thine enemies that rise up against thee to be smitten before thee; one way they shall come out against thee, and seven ways they shall flee from thee. The L-rd will command the blessing with thee in thy barns and in all that thou puttest thy hand unto.**
>
> **The L-ord will establish Thee for a holy people unto himself, as he hath sworn unto thee; if thou shall keep the commandments of the L-rd Thy G-d, and walk in his ways. And all the peoples of the earth shall see that the name of the L-rd is called upon thee; and they shall be afraid of thee...If thou harken unto the commandments of the L-rd Thy G-d which I command thee this day to observe and to do them; and shall not turn aside from any of the words which I command you this day, to the right hand, or the left, to go after other gods to serve them" (such as serving money, power, sexual desires or other forms of idolatry).**

This is the essence of the unique status of the Jewish people as described in the secular as well as the Jewish chronicles. It explains why we have always excelled and stood out from the crowd, (though many of the great Jews in modern history were assimilated), and also why others have been jealous of us. It also explains how we can be protected against the wrath of the multitude, and more recently, how 3 million Israelis can defeat 100 million Arabs.

However, when we forget the source of this power and attribute it to our own egos, then the other side of power is revealed:

> **But it shall come to pass if thou will not harken unto the voice of the L-rd thy G-d to observe to do all his commandments and his statutes which I command thee this day; that all these curses shall come upon thee and overtake thee. The L-rd will send upon thee cursing, discomfiture, and rebuke, and all that thou puttest thy hands unto to do, until thou be destroyed, and until thou perish quickly; because of the evil of thy doings whereby thou hast forsaken me...And the L-rd shall scatter thee among all peoples, from one end of the earth even unto the other end of the earth, and among these nations shall thou have no repose. There shall be no rest for the sole of thy foot; but the L-rd shall give thee there a trembling heart, and failing eyes, and languishing of soul. And thy life shall hang in doubt before thee; and thou shall fear night and day, and shall have no assurance of thy life. In the morning thou shall say: 'Would that it were evening!' and at evening thou shall say: 'Would it were morning!' for the fear of thy heart which thou shall fear, and for the sight of thine eyes which thou shalt see.**

What an incredible description of the facts that we know of the Diaspora and the recent Holocaust! A situation where carcasses were piled up to rot, where people were infested with lice in the death camps, where no nation on earth, even the United States, would open its doors to receive the Jews and acted as if we were a horror unto them. Could this again be some mere coincidence?! Obviously not.

This holocaust is only remarkable for its proximity in our lifetimes and its magnitude. However, there were numerous holocausts in the past such as when the Babylonians, Arabs, Romans, Greeks and other invaded our land and did the same to us. Other Jews were dispersed out of the land of Israel and had to fear for their lives in all other nations to which they fled. In each case, history demonstrates that prior to each holocaust many Jews of the time were becoming assimilated and abandoning their strict observance of the Law of G-d according to the contract that our ancestors bound us to follow. Many of the Jews of Germany felt that they were Germans first, their profession second, and Jews third. Hitler openly declared that he was here to affirm that every Jew is a Jew forever and can never resign from being one of G-d's Chosen People! Hopefully, modern day Jews in the United States and elsewhere will awaken to this reality before G-d needs to send another Holocaust to get our attention!

Similarly, there are some Jews who are afraid to openly declare their Jewishness because of fear of Christian, Moslem and other forms of oppression. History also shows that this approach has always backfired. Trust in G-d, and following His Law, is the only source of protection." ...the L-rd who is my refuge...He will save you from the ensnaring trap...His Truth is a shield and an armor... A thousand may fall at your left side, and ten thousand at your right, but it will not reach you...because you have said 'The L-rd is my shelter.' He will command his Angels on your behalf, to guard you in all your ways." (Psalm 91)

Of course, one could wonder then as to how pious Jews also died in the Holocaust. Here we must consider that all Jews are responsible for one another. When Cain asked, Am I my brother's keeper? (Genesis 4:), the answer was, and still is, *yes*! This is true for mankind in general, but even more so for Jews. Are we not all from one family (the children of Israel)? The individual may receive blessings beyond his merit by association with his Holy brothers and sisters, and the converse is also true. Haven't you seen yourself how the world will blame all Jews for the mistakes of one individual Jew? It is like the story of three men adrift in a rowboat at sea. One of the them starts to drill a hole under his seat. The others scream out in terror, "What are you doing? We'll all drown!" His answer to them is "Don't worry. I'm only making a hole in *my* part of the boat."

Some of the prophecies in the Torah are yet to come, some are written in a vague or allegorical language, and some are very precisely described, and some of them have already unfolded since the time of Moses. One that I know of, in particular, which gives another astounding demonstration of the power of the prophecy of the Torah is written in the last part of the section of Deuteronomy 28 which I mentioned above, and this prophecy came true many years ago. In line 68 it states, "and the L-rd shall bring thee back unto Egypt in ships...and there ye shall sell yourselves unto your enemies for bondmen and for bondwomen, and no man shall buy you." History tells us that the destruction of Jerusalem by the Romans in 70 c.e., both Titus and Hadrian consigned multitudes of Jews to slavery and Egypt received a large proportion of those slaves. The Romans had a fleet in the Mediterranean and transported these Jews back to Egypt in ships. The Roman troops grew weary of slaughtering Jews and at one point 97,000 young prisoners were spared. Those over 17 years were sent to the mines, or to the arenas to fight against gladiators or against wild beasts; those under 17 were sold as slaves; but the market was so glutted that, though offered at nominal prices, none would buy them! Those who remained unpurchased were sent into confinement, where they perished by hundreds and thousands from hunger (commentary from Hertz Pentateuch). Thus we see another prophecy that was written in the Torah 3300 years ago, which was fulfilled 1000 years later, which occurred 2000 years prior to our present time!

One should not think that the Torah has been modified for convenience in this regard. The Torah has not changed one dot on one letter since the time that Moses wrote it. In fact it was our brother Jesus who is quoted in Matthew 5:18-20 as having stated: "Till heaven and earth pass (and as far as I know they're still here!), one jot or one title shall in no wise pass from the Law (Torah), till all be fulfilled. Whosoever therefore shall break one of these least commandments...shall be called the least in the Kingdom of Heaven... that except your righteousness shall exceed the righteousness of the Scribes and Pharisees, ye shall in no case enter into the Kingdom of Heaven."

Most convincing of all should be the "stiff-necked nature" of the Jewish people themselves. The Torah (written law) was recorded by Moses in the presence of the whole nation. He recorded their repeated rebellions, lack of faith, and punishments, as well as observance, faith, rewards and miracles. Do you think that such a people would allow him to write down things that they knew had not happened to them? We are no so different from our ancestors. We have the same stiff necks, lack of faith and rebellion. We would not allow untruths to be recorded in the Torah, and neither did they.

In addition, we know of one very major difference between the teachings of the Torah as opposed to all the other religions of the world. In all cases, there was one spiritual leader who received the word of G-d. But the Torah records that not only did all of the Jewish nation witness the miracles at the Hand of G-d in Egypt, but also all the Egyptians.

I return now to my personal experiences. Several months after moving to Duncan, I made my first trip to Israel. Prior to this I went to Greece and specifically to the location of the Oracle of Delphi in order to take an "energy reading" of the area. I found that it was very beautiful but I senses no presence there. Similarly I went to Egypt to the Pyramids and the tombs of the Pharaohs and found only a very small presence. I then went to the supposed site of Mt. Sinai and found a somewhat larger, yet still only a small Presence. Only much later did I learn that the Holiness of this area was noted in the Torah as being only a transient phenomenon, unlike the Temple Mount which is eternally Holy.

I next went to the Western Wall in Jerusalem and found there an incredible Presence. It was an awesome experience that I do not know how to describe. I felt as if the wall came out and embraced me and my essence merged into it. At that time I was less clear about the necessity to observe the detail of the laws as expressed in the Torah and by the Rabbis, and accepted an invitation by a secular tour group to visit the Dome of the Rock on the Temple Mount. This is the place where Avraham experienced the "near sacrifice" of his son Yitzchak, and is also the place of the Holy of Holies. This is where the Ark and the Ten Commandments received by Moses were kept in the Holy Temple built by King Solomon. It is currently under Moslem control in the Old City of Jerusalem and has a physically beautiful, but spiritually disturbing Moslem building upon it. It is open to visitors but it is not available to Orthodox Jews because of its Holy nature and our inability to properly prepare for it in the absence of the Temple. Nevertheless, I went because I did not fully understand these things. Upon entering this building I saw the bare rock with a guard rail around it, and of course the beautiful building surrounding this. I was immediately overwhelmed by the intensity of the Presence at this site. I felt as if it were pushing upon me, that I was indeed in a truly Holy place, that this was indeed the Holy place of G-d. This was not something that came upon me accidentally or by wishful thinking but was a startling contrast to the other experiences just described–even the Wall and Mt. Sinai!

Upon returning to Duncan, I found myself practicing medicine in a small town and living on a farm with chickens and cows (similar to my great-great grandfathers) and studying the Torah (similar to my great grandfathers) and trying to integrate all this into secular society (similar to my grandfather and father) and hoping to pass all this along to my son (as they all did). I began to see how the timeless forces were interacting, and many of the unanswerable questions of my youth started to fit into place.

I saw that I was physically incarnated at this time, despite forces which opposed it, in order to become an agent of G-d for healing. Thus, I became a physician who teaches people about their physical, mental and spiritual health in addition to attending to their crises. I also did this in a small town in order to complete some of the work which my great grandfathers had begun.

I was destined to be an observant Jew, one of G-d's Chosen, with the obligation of elevating myself and the world to the highest possible level. In this, I am honored to be a member of the tribe of Levi–the only tribe not be have been enslaved in Egypt's workforce nor to have sinned there or at the golden calf; the priestly tribe whose duty was to serve in G-d's Temple.

I could also begin to see how G-d in his great Mercy arranged my *seemingly* traumatic life events in order to guide me back along his path. I was saved from the abortion through G-d's Will, as expressed through the Attributes of Mercy and Kindness, through my mother. I then understood how I had come to the accident that shattered my bones. "Many are the afflictions of a righteous person, but the L-rd rescues him from them all. He protects all his bones, not one of them is broken. Evil brings death upon the wicked…The L-rd redeems the souls of servants." (Psalm 34). I had done things which are accountable by the death penalty according to the strict letter of the Law, yet despite my insufficient spiritually redeeming merits, G-d in his Mercy, saw to restore my Soul and give me another opportunity to follow his path. Some people, such as myself, need to be hit hard over the head before they get the message.

Through increasing awareness, I began to discover the roots and branches of my immortal Soul and what I have to do to nourish it. I saw the value of the Law, both from the practical side of dealing with cows who step in holes, and from an increased perception that the physical detail of the Law is merely a crystallization, in this realm, of the mystical and spiritual force fields of G-d's Creation. I learned that all questions were not meant to be answered, nor all answers to be questioned. For example, instead of seeing the Sabbath as a day which interfered with the things one does during the week, it has become recognized as the major focus of existence, and it is unfortunate that the days of the week interfere with having perpetual Sabbos! This is, in fact, what we are looking for! It is the source of our Soul and we require reunification with it. While we are on this level, the minimum requirement for spiritual survival is once weekly. It is also the ultimate goal individually as well as collectively, and is the essence of the Messianic Era.

At this point in my life I have thus been able to resume an integration of the substance and the form, of the feeling and the knowledge. It has transformed my total outlook on life as well as every moment of how I live it. It appears that there is no life without this connection to G-d. This union is reflected by the famous phrase: "Hear, O Israel: The L-rd our G-d, the L-rd is One (Deuteronomy 6:4). And the concept of living according to G-d's way, and performing His commandments purely out of love for Him, is reflected in my quote from Deuteronomy 6:5-9, "And thou shall love the L-rd Thy G-d with *all* thy heart, and with all thy soul, and with all thy might. And these words, which I command thee this day, shall be upon thy heart. And thou shall teach them diligently unto thy children, and shall talk of them when thou sit in thy house, and when thou walk by the way, and when thy lie down, and when thou rise up. And thou shall bind the for a sign upon the hand (Teffilin), and they shall be for frontlets between thine eyes (Tefillin) and thou shall write them upon the door post of thy house and upon the gates (Mezuzah)." So that your being is totally surrounded by Holiness.

In spite of all that I have attempted to place before you, some of you might still be asking, "What does this man's life story have to do with me?" I will ask you to view the events that I have described as general patterns rather than as my specific entities. Review the path of your own life. Reexamine the "traumatic" events and see if you can reinterpret them in a more meaningful way. Ask yourself where you came from, where you are going, why, and how. What is the goal and purpose of your life? Is it to make money, or build buildings, or have your name up in lights or on many diplomas, or chase women (men)? Are any of these worth going through the difficulties and pains of life? Are we born to have pleasure and pain and then die and that's all?

The quest for power, money, sex, etc, is that toward which most peoples and societies throughout history have invested their life energies. But it has not brought them health, happiness or peace of mind. They are constantly killing themselves and each other over who can get more of these things. They have also been killing Jews (really out of jealousy and fear) because we are different. Instead of chasing after these frivolous things, which are of limited value in This World and on none in the Next, we have had our eyes and hearts directed toward reuniting our External Souls with the Creator.

So what will become of you if the ways of the nations are wrong and the Torah is true? And what will it cost you to live according to the Torah, and what will be the rewards? If you have not yet clarified these issues in your own life, then I would like to invite you to try a "scientific" experiment for yourself. Plan to live, at least in some small way, according to the guidelines of the Torah for a period of time, and see how your life changes. Find someone who observes and loves the Shabbos and share one with them. Think Holy thoughts, eat Holy food, pray and meditate upon your relationship with the Master of the Universe, The Holy One, Blessed be He.

In conclusion I would like to remind us of the prayer which is called Aleinu. It is the closing prayer for morning, afternoon and evening services. It expresses the hope for the day when all people, Jews and non-Jews alike, will recognize the nature of the relationship between man/woman and G-d, and will enter into the Messianic era where there will be peace on earth for all.

Thank you for allowing me the privilege of sharing my insights of G-dliness, Jewishness, and the essence of life with you. If any one wishes to discuss any aspect of this with me, I would be delighted and honored to do so. But in any case, I hope and pray that we may all be able to redirect our life's path to one that is guided by His Light; to discard the usual human fear of giving and receiving love (which is the source of most of our pain) and to re-unite our broken hearts through the Oneness provided by being in the state of love-fear-awe of the Creator. On such a level, one only interacts with their fellow beings in goodness, kindness, wisdom, mercy and love. And I ask the Master of the Universe to allow us to reach and know each other on this level.

> **"May the L-rd bless all of you and guard you.**
> **May He shine His Presence upon you,**
> **and be gracious unto you.**
> **May he elevate you with His Presence**
> **and grant you Peace."**
>
> **(Numbers 6:24-26)**

May the words of my mouth (and typewriter), and the meditations of my heart be acceptable before you, L-rd, my Strength and my Redeemer. (Psalm 19:15) Amen

A Child Raised in Orthodoxy
Clara F. Zilberstein, Ph.D.

A friend once described a seemingly insignificant event which was actually a small turning point in his life. When he was a small child, he was fascinated by the counter of tiny toys in his local five and dime store. He loved the glass dividers that separated the miniatures and always longed to stand in front of that counter. He neither touched nor played with the toys but his mother could leave him standing in front of that counter endlessly and he never tired of staring at those glass dividers and the miniatures within.

He never knew consciously or intellectually what it was that fascinated him; after all, he was only eight years old. But day after day, or as often as he could, this little boy stood in front of the counter, fully captivated. Today he know that there was something numinous about those glass dividers and the miniatures within those dividers. Something touched him and moved him. Something touched his psyche. One day he was taken into Woolworth's and he ran to his beloved counter. On that day, he found the counter no longer of fascination. Whatever held him no longer had an impact on him. Whatever touched the psyche in a magical way was now commonplace and profane. The symbol had lost its numinosity and it ceased to be a symbol. And as soon as that happened, my friend left that counter and never returned.

The ability and spontaneity to follow that which is numinous seems essential to the spiritual experience. Perhaps the spirit is actually revealed in the numinous. The spiritual path, the active relationship to G-d, would then demand an openness to the numen. The individual would have to follow the psychic energy through all of its attachments, trusting the authenticity of the numen, the psychic magnet that stirs an attachment that sometimes defies and sometimes transcends rationality but moves the individual forward in the spiritual journey.

What if the numinous is ignored? A symbol has a gripping effect on an individual and the individual denies that effect. The individual essential ignores the soul. The individual censors the soul, following the conventional path, and not the path of the soul. The instincts are repressed or denied, the instincts which comprise the foundation of the affective or denied, the instincts which comprise the foundation of the affective response to the numinous. Perhaps by so ignoring, the individual keeps out G-d or G-d's presence.

Why would the numinous be ignored? If the experience of the numinous is so profound, and if the attraction is from the soul and initially instinctive and not from the intellect, why would not defend against the numinous symbol? It may be because the experience is so awesome. The desire to flee that which is awesome is seen in the Old Testament, for example, when the children of Israel beg Moses to present them with the Word of the Law because they are awed and fearful of G-d. However, there is no escape from the numinous here. The very attempt to flee validates the presence of G-d in the experience.

The experience of the numinous might be ignored because of feeling unworthy. Raised in Orthodoxy, the child is taught to strive for perfection at the same time knowing there is no perfection. I think one reason the Orthodox tend to lose faith less often when struck by misfortune is because they tend to ask "why me?" less often. In terms of justice and punishment, an Orthodox Jew knows there is always some transgression (s)he is committing and knows there is always something for which punishment can be justified and, if not individually, then surely for the sins of the nation.

Knowing there is always more to strive for, one always feels short of worthy. Although Biblical figures are presented in all their humanness including their shortcomings, the implication of day-to-day teaching is that revelation is not for everyone and that G-d appears to those free of sin and great of understanding.

It is possible to ignore the numen if it happens to fall on a symbol outside the boundaries of Halacha (the Path of the Law). Halacha *is* the numinous within Orthodoxy. It is the living dynamic symbol, the container, the vehicle to G-d. It is through the practice, the doing, that spirituality is experienced for the Orthodox Jew. If the Halacha is not numinous, the Jew must continue to follow Halacha, to live by Halacha. If a symbol is numinous but happens to be outside Halacha or contrary to it, that numinosity must be ignored. The prophet who has visions or revelations which contradict or oppose Halacha is a false prophet.

A child raised in Orthodoxy learns to experience G-d and the spiritual through the container of Halacha alone. There is an inevitable inhibition of the spontaneous following the numinous, an inhibition of the instinctive following of the dart of psychic energy. For the spiritual child much curiosity and seeking is inevitably sacrificed. If the Halacha stays alive and numinous, that child can be contained within it. Sometimes, the Halacha does not stay numinous, certainly a possibility when a rational system is imposed on a intuitive and spiritual child. Naturally, the child feels inadequate and guilty. If, at the same time the Orthodoxy is embraced and honored, the child will find fault with the Self and not with the Halacha, since the Teaching is that the Halacha is infallible and the individual, even the Self, is not. Ironically, the rift between the individual and the Self grows with the desire to close the gap between the Self and G-d. Of course, without the relation to Self, to the instincts, to the ability to follow the numen, there are no tools to further spiritual development. The thirst remains and the only "Kosher" elixir is the Halacha.

My friend's experience in the five and dime touched me deeply. The pattern of his spiritual journey was set. He never dictated the path or direction. He never had a "Halacha," a proscribed way from without. He waited and he listened and he followed. He had, and has, great patience for the journey. He has an unwavering faith. He follows religiously. He has only his instincts, his curiosity, his psychic responses, his soul as his guides.

It is different from the Orthodox child who loves the tradition yet is not wholly contained within it, who does not fully experience the numen of the Halacha, yet cannot open to the numinous from anywhere else because it is met with suspicion and the fear of heretical inauthenticity. The orthodox child waits. The longing is for G-d. The teaching dictates a proscribed way yet the child is full of an original search and direction that must be denied. How the child would love a sign, a sign from G-d. The child feels unworthy of a sign and also a heretic to ask for direction beyond the Halacha, the beloved Halacha. And so, the child waits.

God's Gift To Me

Bertha Miller

I became a Freak. I wasn't the least of one until I reached the age of 36. God gave me the gift of Arthritis. Not just Arthritis, but the real McCoy. Why? I ask myself what did I do? What crime did I commit?

Now I am serving a life sentence just as a murderer would, yet worse, shut in, I hardly see anyone, bedridden and depressed.

I can't describe the pain I have every second of the day or night, for there is no word in the universe for it. I don't want sympathy or pity.

My hands turned to claws.
My toes are twisted.
My knees are useless.
My hip only moves a certain degree.
My back is painful.
My arms are unable to straighten out.
My head is swollen and sore on one side.
My neck is painful. It cracks like someone breaking walnuts.
What have I left? Nothing.

This is not enough for me. There are family problems giving me heart-aches. There is no love, no feeling, no understanding. Is this living? Why go on?

Slowly, I am becoming like a pretzel.

–Bertha Miller, September, 1983, Died March, 1984

Gender Politics and The Soul
A Jewish Feminist Journey
Gloria Feman Orenstein, Ph.D.

A Tu B'Shvat Seder For The Trees at the home of Savina Teubal, author of Sarah The Priestess[1]. We women do not know each other, but we have come a long way in order to celebrate our emergence from the winter of our spirits to a new cycle of rebirth into Jewish feminist culture. Fern has brought leaves and thread for us to make ritual decorations. Savina has set the table with fine crystal for the ceremony of mixing the wines from white to red symbolizing our leaving Winter for the communal pot-luck. Some of us, Irene and I, have brought along our children. Others have invited friends. Bruria, and Israeli artist, and Savina, our hostess, read Hebrew fluently. Later they enter into a heated debate about certain stories in the Bible which Savina has reinterpreted in her book, concluding that Judaism originally had another strain, a matricentric lineage as well as a patriarchal one. It descends from Sarah, who may well have been a Priestess of the Goddess religion. Sarah, who spent most of her life in a sacred grove of terebinth trees at Mamre, may even have taken an oath not to bear children, as did many women of her time who were Priestesses. Thus, her "infertility" or what is often referred to as her "barrenness" is probably a clue to her true identity as a Priestess.

The idea that Sarah could have been a Priestess of the Goddess religion thrills me. For many years now I have been a scholar of

Comparative Literature and the Arts, studying women and creation, and I have been constantly preoccupied by one image–that of the reemergence of the Goddesses in art and literature by contemporary women. Yet, as a Jewish woman I feel both guilty for being obsessed by my search for the Goddess, and, simultaneously ecstatic about discovering that our most ancient matriarch may even have revered Her.

Our Seder begins. We light candles, say prayers, read poetry, share our writings, our dreams for this evening, for this world, for ourselves, our families, our friends, and we eat the two best kugels we have tasted since our childhood. We explain the fine art of the Ashkenazi Kugel to Savina whose background is Safardic. Some of us speak in Jungian terms about our inner searches for the integration of the "masculine" and the "feminine" within ourselves, assuming that others now exactly what we mean by those labels. Others of us react vehemently to this vocabulary and its ideological implications. "Haven't we learned that 'masculine' and 'feminine' are social constructions?" we ask. "Haven't we proved through a decade of feminist scholarship in a variety of disciplines that gender roles vary from culture to culture?" "No!" claim the Jungians. "We feel ourselves to be deeply 'feminine,' and moving towards an integration with our 'masculine' counterparts within the self as we become more independent, as we learn to participate in the creation of our own culture and the transformation of society." We must above all be patient with each other, I think, as my voice pierces the hallowed space of communion and rises shrilly to contest: "No, you are wrong! We do not have 'masculine selves' or 'aspects' of the self. We are women and our independence is female. What you are calling 'masculine' in you I call 'female' in me.

We have been going at each other for two hours–about whether Sarah could have been a Priestess of the Goddess religion, about gender and socialization, about inner guides and spiritual revelations, about transformation and Feminism. As we recite our own prayers to each other, and as we tell each other about our studies and about our life experiences I suddenly feel intensely that we are women passionately engaged in a search for God or Goddess, a search for our origins–that we are women's Yeshiva might feel like. But, as women, we do not have our own scrolls to argue about, so we are disputing our recent scholarship as we would dispute a sacred text. We have already written some of our own stories, our own commentaries, our own "midrash," and as we do so, we are creating our own tradition!" But is this Jewish?" we continually ask ourselves.

Last week we attended Adrienne Rich's talk on Jewish women poets at U.C.L.A. Marcia Falk, our friend, and poet-scholar in Los Angeles, is writing new prayers which say: "Let us now bless the wine, the fruit of the vine, etc." Instead of Blessed art thou O Lord our God, King of the Universe." But, "Is it Jewish?" we ask ourselves again and again. Marcia's reply is always: "I'm deeply Jewish. I've studied Jewish tradition all my life. Of course it's Jewish. But it's also inclusive of women." We ask her if the Rabbis, even the women Rabbis think it's Jewish. I ask Rabbi Patti Karlin Newman of U.C.L.A., if, as one of the first women Rabbis in the history of Judaism, she couldn't simply make a pronouncement saying: "We women Rabbis recognize the pain and struggle of contemporary Jewish women to write women experiences into Jewish prayer and scholarship, and we recognize their new prayers, their new art, and their new scholarship as profoundly Jewish." I tell her how much anguish it would save us to know that what we dream and creates as Jewish women is, in fact, recognized as Jewish. She replies that she has the authority to make such a pronouncement, and, indeed, she would make it if she were convinced it were Jewish. "But Gloria," she responds, "we have been over this many times. Your Goddess is simply not Jewish. We have to make distinctions somewhere; to draw the line between what is and what isn't Jewish. We can't accept everything as Jewish."

Adrienne Rich has been telling us how she struggled with her Jewish identity–not ever thinking that the Bible her Jewish father read to her as a child was the "Jewish Bible."

How did we come to this time and place? How did we come to the Seder of the Trees, as feminists, from the ceremony of "Creating A Home For Our Scrolls" that grew out of the "Shekinah" conference? Why is it that my response to the topic "The Modern Jew in Search of Soul" is the story of Jewish feminist rituals and conferences, of communal rather than one of revelations, illuminations and dreams? Is it because for so long women have been identified with community in Judaism that we have, once more, automatically reenacted our traditional roles? Or is it because having come full circle, through entry into male-identified spheres such as those of study and prayer, we feel that our "feminist" values must place a higher priority upon human connectedness, now that we are entering an age of high technology and intensified alienation?

I have come to Los Angeles from New York and I often tell people that the change has marked, for me, an entry into the world of the future and of the machine. In New York we are surrounded by people packed into elevators and subways like sardines, engulfed by crowds everywhere we go. Here, in Los Angeles, we spend the day alone in our cars, listening to tapes, or at home with answering machines, computers, video cassette recorders, more tapes...When we shop a computerized voice, like a disembodied ghost, rises from the cash register and announces the price of what we have purchased. Because of this technical pollution we crave community and society more than ever. We yearn for human passion, for the flame and zeal of commitment to ideals and the energized emotional atmosphere that poetry, philosophy and art generate. Our endless robotics, artificial intelligences, plastic ready-made-foods, drive-in computerized electronic life-styles and games, Pac-Man and Pac-Woman, all the simulacra of life deprives us of contact with the vital forces of nature and the characteristics of human though that defy computer programs such as humor and ambiguity, sources of creativity.

And so we come to this time, 1985, to this place, Santa Monica Savina Teubal's house surrounded by fruit trees, to shed the winter of our souls and enter a period of communal rebirth symbolized by the Tree of Life that Tu B'Shvat commemorates.

All of this began when I was appointed to the Planning Committee of the Shekinah Conference. I was to represent U.S.C.'s Program for The Study of Women and Men in Society in which I teach. Our conference was to be about Jewish women and spirituality, and our first discussion centered on the title: Did we mean women's spirituality in Jewish tradition or women's spirituality **and** Jewish tradition? I fought for **and**, because it seemed to me that my own spirituality which had been loosely referred to as "pagan" until then because of its association with the "goddess" seemed to be defined as "outside" the realm of the Jewish religion. Yet, I felt deeply Jewish, and was reminded of my Jewishness all the time by my feminist sisters of other religions. It held no water with them whether I confessed to my former atheism, my flirtation with Buddhism, my discovery of the Goddess. For them I was Jewish, and that was that! But the Rabbis had other opinions in the matter.

We called our conference "Illuminating The Unwritten Scroll: Women's Spirituality *and* Jewish Tradition," and we took the name of "Shekinah" for our all-embracing symbol. The unwritten scroll represented for us the Torah as it might have been, had women written it.

I was to do a workshop on the Goddess with Anthropologist, Gelya Frank. At last I would pose the question of the goddess' re-emergence in contemporary art to Jewish women. At last I would know whether my goddess had anything to do with Judaism. As I prepared for the workshop I reflected upon my life and my Jewish background. As a child I had attended temple regularly on holidays. I was confirmed at 13, as was the custom in my era, and I attended Brandeis University, graduating in its 8th graduating class. Having lived in N.Y. and attended Brandeis, I was virtually unfamiliar with anti-Semitism. However, I did marry a Holocaust survivor from France, and although I was sympathetic to his sufferings as a child during the Holocaust, I also analysed the Sexism within my cultural tradition as I experienced it in marriage. Why did I identify it as Jewish? I have been faulted for this. Everyone reminds me that the Sexism I associate with Judaism is rampant in patriarchy, in general. I suppose that I had expected Jews to rise above all forms of discrimination, having suffered from one virulent form of it themselves. I was naive about how wounds are transmitted from generation to generation.

After my marriage ended, after I received my doctorate and had searched for spiritual meaning in various arenas such as the occult, the mystical, magical, I found myself telling people that I was only a secular Jew; spiritually I felt attracted to a Goddess religion. It had been anti-Semitism that originally sensitized me to Sexism, but in my more recent involvement with Feminism I had come full cycle, and once more encountered anti-Semitism. Thus, I came to a point where I wanted to resolve all the political conflicts in my identity. I wanted to find a way to be both Jewish and Feminist.

I was also a feminist activist, co-creating a literary salon for women writers in New York which lasted over 10 years thanks to my cofounder Erika Duncan, who was also Jewish. It was known as The Woman's Salon, and as I did research on Jewish women in history I learned that created literary salons was precisely what they did in the past–especially in Germany where there is a long legacy of Jewish salon women like Rachel Varnhagen, who assimilated to mainstream of literary and intellectual life through their salons.

Thus I was living out a pattern that other intellectual Jewish women had lived before me. But none of them had ever turned to the Goddess for spiritual sustenance. Robert M. Seltzer, in his book *Jewish People Jewish Though: The Jewish Experience in History*[2] tells us that "Radical Monotheism, the principle that there exists but one God, is the contribution of biblical Israel to Western civilization. Israel was the first monotheistic people in the world at a time when polytheism was the norm." "The crucial moment in the emergence of Israelite monotheism, therefore, was the decision that 'other gods are idols,' the work of men's hands, artifacts of human culture. Yahweh was not 'a god' but GOD, a being whose nature is unique, absolute and ultimate."[3] The god of the Hebrews was also, we are told, genderless, transcendent, limitless, and imageless. Yet, we know that this God has been transmitted to us gendered as a Father God. I wondered if any of these Jewish women from our history had felt the need for a different image of God, or had ever wondered why Monotheism was superior to Polytheism, in principle.

My research has shown that contemporary women of vision (artists both Jewish and non-Jewish) have in fact been reevoking the Goddess as a symbol of our new feminist consciousness, of our erased pre-history and history, of our rebirth into a new era in which women name reality for themselves. Contemporary women artists and writers use it as a symbol of the reclamation of their own creative abilities and of a reverence for nature as well as, of course, a reaffirmation of female procreation. These are just some of the meanings of the reemergence of the Goddess in women's culture today. It is in general a symbol of the knowledge of women's history and of the power that comes from that knowledge.

Paradoxically this goddess symbol is usually not that of a deity per se. It does not denote a monotheistic belief structure as opposed to a polytheistic one (with female counterparts of male gods). In fact, it does not speak about religion with a dogma. It speaks about a non-dogmatic spirituality, going back to a first-hand encounter with a dimension of spiritual experience, be it in a cave where once the goddess was revered in Neolithic times, or the experience of the land as sacred, the female as sacred, the sexual as sacred, life, itself as sacred.

As I write this I am aware that I experience a very deep taboo in saying that I am asking myself if there is anything superior about monotheism, about any theism that empowers males at the expense of females. In view of the oppression that centuries of Jewish women have experienced in our monotheism, I do not feel that those cultures which had a plurality of gods, some of which were goddesses, were inferior. It is heresy for me to say this. I know it, yet, I must say this as a Jewish woman who was alienated by patriarchal monotheism.

In her book *Ancient Mirrors of Womanhood*[4] Merlin Stone talks about the negative effects that various aspects of the Jewish Religion (as well as other patriarchal religions) can have upon women. She shows, referring to goddesses from other cultures, such as those mentioned in creation stories by the Akkadians, the Sumerians, the Indians, the Australians, the Chinese, the Egyptians, the Native Americans, the Cretans, etc., that refer to these beliefs as mere "mythology" or to label them as "heathen" or "pagan" is to ignore a long history in which the deity and the clergy were female.

Merlin Stone told us, too, that for 35 centuries after the initial period of writing developed in the Jemdet Nsr period of Sumer, in 3200 BCE, the goddess was not only revered, but honored in written tablets and papyri. We know, through the works of Archeologist Marija Gimbutas[5] that from 7,000 BCE and as far back as 25,000 BCE, before writing, the goddess was also revered by ancient people of Old Europe.

We might ask ourselves, as contemporary Jews, what makes our creation mythology, on that has no goddesses, more valid, superior, more spiritual or more important? High priestesses, goddesses, and woman shamans are familiar images to women raised in many of the cultures of the world. As a Jewish woman I was told that we were superior because our God was transcendent, genderless, and imageless. Then, in the very next breath I was told about Him, about God the Father. I now realize how impoverished I have been–deprived as I was of the potent examples of female strength encoded in the image of the female creatress, the images of female power, of female energy, and of female priestesses that women of other cultures know and contemplate as they grow.

While I joyfully celebrate the acceptance of women to the Rabbinate, I am still denied a female aspect of the deity. Merlin Stone shows that the goddesses worshipped by people in a variety of cultures did not symbolize just one thing, but represented a multitude of aspects, traits, and powers.

Moon, sun, stars, volcanoes, rivers, lakes, trees, corn, bird, Queen of Heaven and Mother Earth, lawgivers, compassionate one, wrathful one, holy ones, wise ones, symbols of liberty, justice, victory, warrior women, hunters, ancestors, mothers, guardians, scribes…all of these have been symbols, roles and images of goddesses, of women.

Why have the many accounts of these goddesses been suppressed and erased? What do they mean for Jewish women today who find their own theology too patriarchal? As Jews we are probably most interested in the accounts of the Goddess Asherah. Why was the once-sacred image of woman then degraded? Why was the reverence of Her referred to as a cult, as a myth rather than as a religion that lasted over 3500 years–perhaps longer than 7,000 years? Merlin Stone also sees the connection between Goddess reverence and the sanctity of nature. She sees the fact that womanhood was held as sacred among people who revered a goddess, be they Mexican, Irish, or Zuni, as very important. In reading her I ask myself again and again, as a Jewish woman, what would I write into Judaism to meet this need that I have for the dimension of spirituality that the Goddess symbol has represented in terms of empowering women, a dimension that embraces both nature and culture in a positive way? At my workshop I show slides of art by women both Jewish and non-Jewish, such as the Jewish artists Miriam Sharon (Israel), Judy Chicago, Rachel Rosenthal, Susan Schwalb, Helene Aylon, Ruth Weisberg, Ghila Yelin Hirsch, Beth Ames Swartz, Ana Homler, and the non-Jewish artists Ana Mendieta, Mary Beth Edelson, Helene de Beauvoir, Betsy Damon, Jovette Marchessault, Leonara Carrington.

While the non-Jewish artists seem to connect the goddess with earth energies and the realm of animals and nature, the works of Jewish artists often relate their Goddess references to the spiritual dimension within history, both secular and sacred, communal and personal. Judy Chicago's *Dinner Party* is an excellent example of this kind of search for a transcendent spiritual community of women. Esther Broner's novel *A Weave of Women*[6] is about a Jewish feminist community in Jerusalem. Ruth Weisberg's art is concerned with our relationship to the host of Jewish souls who have lived and died before us, whose lives and spirit we commemorate in our own lives and works.

In our workshop Gelya Frank leads the audience on a guided imagery journey and asks them to name the deity they encounter, to tell: where it comes from, what it looks like, whether it is accompanied, what its gifts are, what it wants of us, how it envisages women's role in Judaism in the future. Our responses are amazing! The women present envisage either a female being or an intensely warm and brilliant light. Three of them name her "Jane." "What does that mean?", we continually ask ourselves. "Why Jane?" We laugh. We feel guilty for taking this seriously. Even for having done it. But we secretly want to repeat it until we collect evidence about whether Jewish women image the deity as female and if so, what she represents to them.

Our conference had so many high moments that 350 evaluations handed in out of about 550 women attending said it was the best conference ever attended.

During the program Blu Greenberg shared her personal struggle with us–that of a traditional Jew married to a Rabbi and the mother of five children who encounters feminism. Deena Metzger meditated upon how "the destruction of our world may have to do with when the spirit was separated from women." She asked: "How do you learn to walk that path where you find the temple even if it's inside your heart?" Ruth Weisberg talked about the prohibition against making graven images and icons and the effect that has had upon Jewish art. She showed the work of many of the same Jewish artists whose works I study, and named them as the first generation to make a new Jewish art. Her own life in art is "a commemorative journey." She bonds with the children of the holocaust and the people of the Shtetl, as if her art could hold them back from their fate. She feels intensely connected to the past and to the cycle of life that began before her birth and extends into the future beyond her death and into "the world to come," when all the Jews who have ever lived will be present in the host of multitudes. That night is one of the workshops I write in my journal: "Is it too late to return to a Jewish identity? Do I care to belong to a religion that for centuries has oppressed my own people, women? Can the goddess be a part of contemporary Jewish and spiritual experience? Why do I need a goddess rather than a genderless symbol–a light, a Star of David, or Sarah? Do I need a Mother now that my own mother has died?

Later Rachel Adler mounted "the women who suffered excision," our foremothers, who were erased from our history. She exclaimed: "This oppression stops here with me!" For Rachel Adler, it is our exclusion from God's image that makes us feel that "this is Egypt." She asked: "Can women be Jews?" and she concluded "Jewish women have not transgressed by being oppressors." "Our abuse in Judaism is painful, enraging–we must own this painful story...salvage what is salvageable and build forward."

To hear these women raise their voices–articulate, educated, passionate, angry voices, is, for me, to commune with the very heart of Jewish Feminism. These women seem to embody the spirit of the Kabbalah, from which we derive the word "cabbale."

Then I hear Ellen Umansky saying: "Can the divine be Goddess if idolatry is to worship a Goddess?" "Can we appropriate the Goddess?" I hear her saying: "This is important."

Why do all women cry when Marcia Falk tries to write a blessing, and in taking images seriously, as a poet should, rejects the male image and grammar of God? Why are we afraid this is not Jewish? We are accused of Paganism when we change the image of God. She asks if any single image could ever possibly include us all. She says that our Monotheism is merely idol worship if we don't understand that we need multiple images in an infinite variety in order to name God. Marcia says: "Let us bless the source of life," it is the source of life that enables us to grow. We are uplifted and exalted by this new women's Bracha. We feel a rush of emotion, but our tears are those of joy, for at last we are included in the Blessing.

Barbara Meyerhoff was terminally ill with cancer when she spoke to us at the Shekinah Conference. She died a few months later. Barbara spoke to us about ritual and taught us how it helps us to experience the invisible world of our mythic origins. She taught us how ritual makes things sacred, and how it gives form to chaos. She paused to take deep breaths because the conference was one of her life-rituals, and our life-rituals fill us with the very breath of life. As a scholar, too, I recognized this, that the conference, itself, was helping to heal the pain. She looked beautiful and healthy on that particular day, and she was focused, brilliant, lucid, penetrating, as always. We were trembling, for as she spoke she embodied the mystery of life's consciousness of its own fragility. Her talk was her way of helping us to understand our priorities on our own journeys through Jewish history, which we and she were transforming and recasting.

Finally, Esther Broner created a ritual for us with which we closed the conference. We were all gathered together in a large auditorium when Esther appeared on stage in her yarmulke, with Aviva Cantor who was singing a "nigun." Our women rabbis, Laura Geller and Patti Karlin Newman were, coincidentally, wearing white that day. They did not know beforehand that later that evening they would be "married" to the scrolls which Esther had prepared for us. As soon as we saw the scrolls we were all seized with a similar "fury" and were this not about Judaism, I would have to describe it as Dionysiac. Six large scrolls were unfurled before us on the floor of Hebrew Union College's auditorium. Immediately, all those present threw themselves on the floor in order to inscribe words, prayers, blessings, thoughts of love and memories into the scrolls which would then be preserved by Jewish women forever. When the inscription phase of the ceremony was completed, we were given candles, and we paraded out onto the lawn, carrying the scrolls high above our heads. We trailed off into the night singing, dancing, laughing and celebrating. Possessed by the ancient rhythms of Jewish forebears, we then returned to the auditorium and spontaneously "married" our women rabbis to the scrolls, lifting them up in the air in chairs, as is customary in Jewish weddings.

We did the Hora long into the night, and we clung to each other, yearning to live on in the ecstasy of this, our new feminist naming of women's spirituality.

Throughout the ceremony Esther Broner's parents and brother beamed upon her proudly as did Deena Metzger's mother, who had spoken earlier in the day during Starhawk's ritual workshop.

No, we could not bear to return to a world without spiritual ecstasy and sisterhood. What kind of strange wedding was this? Were we spontaneously discovering the roots of some ancient ceremony" We were ritually imploring our high "priestesses" to honor and transmit our communal memories from generation to generation? Were we sanctifying our living history? Suddenly we realized that we absolutely had to make a permanent home for our scrolls!

A few months later I found myself at a meeting of the original Planning Committee of the Shekinah Conference. It had been called because we received a groundswell of public acclaim for us to carry the spirit of Shekinah Conference forward.

Those of us who want to do so met frequently at the Fairfax Council House with Shoshana Hirsch Yom Tov, and came up with the idea of creating a ritual and networking celebration for all those interested in creating a Home for the Scrolls. The Home would be the library of the Fairfax Council House. Fern would prepare a velvet cover for the six scrolls, and we would all bring ornaments, photos, and personal items with which to adorn the scroll covers. I made a journey to the basement of Hebrew Union College in order to retrieve the plexiglass case that had held the scrolls on the stage during our closing ritual. I made it over there just in time, for the case was about to be thrown away in the garbage that very afternoon.

On January 13, 1985, we gathered at the Fairfax Council House for our second ceremony. We opened the scrolls and read excerpts from them. A few weeks earlier I had attended the funeral of Barbara Meyerhoff where Deena Metzger had delivered a moving eulogy, and I wanted to dedicate our ceremony to Barbara's memory and to link it with Esther Broner's ritual. She and Esther had spoken in the same session at the Shekinah Conference.

I wrote the following text which I read at the event where we ceremoniously decorated the scrolls, read from them, and carried them into the library in a dance pattern that had been choreographed for us by Ilene Serlin.

We are forming The Society of Sarah Salon to discuss the ways in which Sarah's values are directly linked to our own. Savina tells us that Sarah was against circumcision. Perhaps we derive from her in our fierce stance against all forms of violence.

One of us comes from Quebec. She is passionately anticlerical. She loves the intensity of our discussion, but cannot stand the subject matter. "Why a spirituality salon at all when so many people are starving, being killed, raped and violated all over the world?" she asks. Every time we pronounce the name of a deity she shudders in order to release the anxiety it provokes in her stemming from her rigid Catholic background. She also practices Co-counseling. We speak about our spiritual journeys. She trembles and shakes on purpose! She has been taught to do this to release tension and discharge anxiety. She is a Socialist-Feminist. It is not that we have turned against Socialist-Feminism, it is just that we have a wild desire to reclaim the entirety of our rightful spiritual heritage. "Why must we make a link to Sarah anyway?" asks one of us. "We can continue our struggle towards non-violence, towards a reverence for life without belonging to the Sarah tradition." "Why do we need this when it is all speculative, hypothetical?" "Can't we simply act on our own behalf without linking our values to those of Sarah?" We ponder this question for a while. It's true. But we have all been doing just that for a decade, and we have come here because we needed something else; we needed our roots and our tradition. "There is power in tradition and there is knowledge in power. If we have knowledge of our legacy, we will have reclaimed that power." We heave a communal sigh in assent. Indeed! We had forgotten. Knowledge is power, and what we Jewish women were lacking was the knowledge of our female heritage. Heritage? Heresy. As I pronounce the very words I feel pangs of guilt. Why your **own** heritage? Is not the heritage of Abraham's legacy sufficient for you? No, it is not! Not for those of us who choose frequent the Society of Sarah Salon, who choose to root our action-in-the-world in Jewish sources, and who have now, for the first time, the possibility of doing so. Why? Because Judaism is a religion which celebrates the history of a people's liberation from slavery, of a people's quest to worship God in their own way. Is this not, then, what we are also doing as we reclaim Sarah, as we reclaim the Goddess Asherah? We, too, are celebrating our Herstory, we are asking to worship God/Goddess in our own language. If it exists, how does one view Stein's Cow-Goddess?

Can this be Jewish? I feel it to be so deeply Jewish that I often wish it were less so. When? When I discuss my Gertrude Stein paper with a writer friend, telling her that if you listen closely for Yiddish in her abstract poetry, you will discover an anti-Seder, and underneath that you will discover a goddess-centered world in which nature and forbidden love are celebrated. You will discover a completely new interpretation of the Garden of Eden (at Bilignin), of forbidden fruit as well. My materialist feminist friend says to me: "Gloria, I cannot dispute what you say, but it's not my thing!" I wish it were less Jewish when I submit my Goddess paper to a contemporary American Feminist journal of materialist persuasion, and they reject it saying that they admire it, but it is simply not their thing. This thing that is not theirs–what is it? It can't be an overt Judaism, because my paper on the Goddess is anything but Jewish. I will call it "soul," for lack of a better word. Whatever it is, it doesn't process, and it is a part of me that feels like it comes from my Jewish background. Soul. Is it that Soul does not process? Is there a sexual politics of the soul, too?

I have been told that I am reclaiming my Jewish identity for the wrong reasons–because of anti-Semitism.

I flash back to the International Women's Studies Conference held in Montreal in July, 1982. The war was raging in Lebanon, and one of the scholars from Lebanon could not come to the conference. A scholar from Morocco who was present read a manifesto denouncing the policies of Israel. There was wild applause. Then there was stamping and cheering. When the Israeli woman spoke to this issue, the manifesto was re-read. Everyone in the room stood up except for about three of us. I remained seated. I was terrified as I observed the sisters with whom I had previously felt a solidarity ask for the dissolution of the State of Israel. It was not that I agreed with the Israeli policies. It was that I remembered of how our people struggled to obtain a homeland for so many centuries after all our exiles, after the Inquisition, after the Holocaust.

I had a sudden realization whether or not I approved of the governmental policies of Israel, I was completely implicated in this issue. I was considered Jewish whether I believed in a Goddess or not; whether the women Rabbi thought I was too "pagan" for Judaism or not. It would be in vain that I would try to explain the subtle nuances of my feminist quest to anyone present in that room.

I had a sudden realization. Whether or not I approved of the governmental policies of Israel, I was completely implicated in this issue. I was considered Jewish whether I believed in a Goddess or not; whether the women rabbis thought I was too "pagan" for Judaism or not. It would be in vain that I would try to explain the subtle nuances of my feminist quest to anyone present in that room.

I had contested Judaism because of its Sexism. I had turned to the pre-patriarchal Goddess instead. Then, Judaism rejected me because of my unorthodox spiritual and political quests. I was equally rejected by my feminist sisters and by my Jewish sisters and brothers, either because of Israeli politics or feminist politics. I was caught in a double bind.

I began to feel that I had no where to turn. When I came back to Los Angeles, I consulted Rabbi Laura Geller, who suggested that we form a Jewish women's faculty group to pursue the discussion of these matters further–which we did.

Three years later we had the Shekinah Conference, The Ritual Creating a Home for The Scrolls, The Seder of The Trees and The Society of Sarah Salon.

It is now clear to me that when we talk about the soul we are entering into a discussion of gender politics again.

As a feminist I must critique the ideological presuppositions inherent in both Jung's work and Judaism. Yet, I have passed through both at different times and have been greatly enriched by what they offered me. What attracts me to both bodies of thought and belief is the notion of the Soul. What I cannot accept is their approach to the concept of gender, which ultimately applies to their concepts of the Soul, as well. If gender is socially constructed and relative, not absolute, then ideas of the "feminine" and the "masculine" are relative and socially constructed as well. Perhaps the soul is also a social construction. While certain attributes are represented by goddesses in one society, it is god who embodies those same qualities in another culture.

Then, in view of this reasoning, why do I insist upon a female image of the Goddess as the creator of life? If it is all cultural relative and socially constructed, should I be satisfied with a genderless image? A male-female dyadic image? Yet, there is something in me that rebels against these two solutions. Reasonable people say that since it is beyond our power to name the Creator, a genderless image, such as a geometric shape or a light should suffice. Yet, gender arrangements, as we know, reflect politics and reinforce power in the secular world. It is probably not until the structures change in the secular world that I would turn to another symbol system. For, even an image of equality can be abused in order to mystify us, and force us into believing that is divine manifestation of equality legislates equality on earth when actually inequality reigns. Isn't it obvious how the blatant contradiction of the Male-god image has already legitimated male-supremacy? It is just amazing how long it took us to notice.

In this matter, I will trust the artists, and when their symbolism changes, I will believe that our secular structures have been undergoing transformation as well. For, I contend that the only reason the Goddess is reappearing in the art and literature of contemporary women is that feminist research has transmitted that knowledge to us–knowledge of our ancient pre-history and of our true legacy from the past. It is this knowledge that we have acquired through research that has stimulated the creative imagination of women artists today. I strongly maintain that to espouse the idea that a "feminine archetype" is re-emerging in our consciousness is to erase the important contribution of feminist scholars to our thought and to obscure both the relationship of knowledge to creation and the relationship of knowledge to imagination. It is at the nexus of feminist scholarship and gender politics that my "search for a Jewish soul" can be situated.

Traditionally, the "search for soul" has been associated with an inner spiritual journey whose pathway could be charted by paying close attention to one's dreams, both on a psychological and a prophetic level. That is approach has caused a problem for me should be obvious by now. This is why I would like to close with a reminiscence about a particularly striking set of dreams I had in 1974 as I was embarking on my career as a university Professor and simultaneously getting a divorce.

All three dreams in this series were about birth, and I'm sure that they would probably be analyzed as dreams in which I gave birth to myself in a new, independent, and creative role.

In the first dream, I was pregnant, and had to get to the hospital to deliver my baby immediately. I told my husband to call a taxi in a hurry, which he did, but he directed the driver to let me off at a battlefield, and I had to deliver among the wounded and the war victims. It was a brutalizing experience, and some of the symbolism of the imagery, such as the battlefield, the war, and the victims van be related to what the end of my marriage felt like.

In the second dream I was also pregnant and had to give birth immediately, but this time I called the taxi myself, and had it drive me safely to a hospital where I could give birth in relative comfort. I also dismissed my husband, because I was afraid he would take me back to the battleground to have the child. In other words, I finally took charge of the situation, gave up the dependence on a man, and gave birth in my own way.

The final dream in the series took place after I had given my lecture at **The Women of Surrealism** at the University of Wisconsin's Center for XXth Century Studies in Milwaukee. It was one of my first public lectures on a topic that I had originated. Although I was ill and feverish, as I was all that winter, I was determined to give the slide-presentation. It was the year of the 50th anniversary of the publication of *The Manifestos of Surrealism*, and I was the only one working on The Women of Surrealism. It was important for me to give this information visibility. So I went to Milwaukee in a terrible blizzard, but I gave a very successful lecture. After the lecture I stayed up all night talking with French writer, Christine Rochefort, who had also come to Milwaukee for Women's Week.

That night I dreamed again that I was pregnant, and that I had to deliver because once more I was in labor. Again I called the taxi myself, and asked to be driven to a hospital of my own choice. As soon as the baby was born I jumped off the delivery table and said to the doctor and the nurses in attendance: "I'm going now. You keep the baby. I have very important work to do in the world. Good-bye."

I did look at it, and I could not believe what I saw! It was a Buddha-child, a male, with an aura around its head, and its legs crossed in the lotus position (or was it the foetal position?) They kept saying to me "It's yours. You'll surely want to keep it! It's a baby!" I stared at it for a long time, and realized that I did want to keep it, that I wanted desperately to keep this child that I had given birth to. I forgot to mention two things. The baby had the head of a very old man. Also, a male friend of mine in New York had a similar dream during that period of time.

The next day I told the dream to several people, all of whom concluded that it meant that I was giving birth to myself. The analysis I had used in my presentation on the Women of Surrealism was Jungian. Many people were very excited by all of this, and, at that time, I was too. I found it to be both fascinating and comforting. In other words, I had given birth to a divine child which was the symbol of my new self as an older, wiser person.

But this was the image of a male! While I realized that women do give birth to males, I did not see how a male image could be an adequate image of me! I knew that it could have represented my "animus" as they say, or some other aspect of the self that, perhaps because of its association with a public role (that of Professor), I might have internalized as male in the patriarchal society in which I was raised.

However, I felt ambivalent about it then, and I do even more so now. If I internalized the image of a divine child as me, it was because that is the way the image had been transmitted to me through Western Art. Once in the Brera Museum in Milan I had been so overcome by the multiplicity of images of Mother and Child in which, of course, the child was always male, that I ran through the museum in flight. As a mother of two daughters, and a daughter myself, I could not identify with the absence of images of a female child. Thus I would now have to join Rachel Adler in proclaiming: "This oppression stops here with me!"

We can finally begin to see the origins of my early obsession with the Goddess in art and literature by contemporary women. I now understand women's creation of this image as a CONSCIOUS choice rather than an unconscious act, such as my dream of the divine male child had been. This conscious creation of images that will circulate in the culture will provide women with reflections of those aspects of themselves that they feel to be sacred, divine, or in the image of the Creator. In the future when women dream that they are giving birth to the creative aspect of themselves they may at last be able to dream that they are giving birth to the daughter of a Goddess, or even to the Goddess, herself.

Today as I finish writing this I attend the Women's History Week Conference in Santa Monica College where there is a panel of women in the clergy. They announce that because it is Saturday, the Jewish women contacted had to decline the invitation to participate in the conference because of the Sabbath. Women ministers from the Catholic, Protestant, and Unitarian Churches talk about their life-stories and their feminist politics. Reverend Carlyle Gill of St. Christopher's By The Sea in Ocean Park, announces that recently someone asked her why she wasn't a Priestess instead of a Minister. This question has led her to begin a personal journey of questioning, research and discovery–a journey into pre-Judeo-Christian religions, and a study of women's roles in them. She says that she images Sarah's circle rather than Jacob's ladder. Click! I take her card, for I will invite her to The Society of Sarah Salon. Perhaps one day women of different faiths will come together in Pre-patriarchal goddess spirituality which will acknowledge the creative aspect of their identity as female. If so, I will be among them. And my hope is that when my own daughters dream realizing their most creative selves in the public world, they will not dream they have given birth to a Buddha-child that they almost reject because they do not recognize it as a symbol for the self, but that they dream of giving birth to an aspect of Asherah. This is not only my most fervent wish, it is my prayer.

REFERENCES

1. Savina Teubal, *Sarah The Priestess*. (Athens, Ohio, Swallow Press, 1984).
2. Robert M. Seltzer, *Jewish People Jewish Thought: The Jewish Experience In History*. (New York: MacMillan, 1980).
3. Ibid.
4. Merlin Stone, *Ancient Mirrors of Womanhood: Our Goddess and Heroine Heritage*. (New York: New Sibylline Books, 1979).
5. Marija Gimbutas. *Goddess and Gods of Old Europe: 6500-3500 BC: Myths and Cult Images*. (Berkeley & L.A.: U of Cal. Press, 1982).
6. Ester Broner. *A Weave of Women*. (New York: Bantam Books, 1978).

How I Learned Judaism at West Point

William A. Cohen, Major General USAF, Ret; Ph.D.

When I was four years old in 1941, the Japanese attacked Pearl Harbor. President Roosevelt immediately asked Congress for a Declaration of War and received it. The U. S. was not strong militarily. With an army of only 174,000 soldiers when rearmament started, the U.S. army ranked 19th in size in the world, right behind Portugal. Except for carriers which had been on maneuvers and out of port, the Pacific Fleet had just been sunk almost in its entirety at Pearl Harbor during the attack. Japan was Germany's ally. Moreover, many powerful and prominent Americans opposed U.S. involvement in a European war and even supported Hitler. These included Charles Lindbergh, Joseph Kennedy, and Henry Ford. Hitler had already defeated other democracies and only England still opposed him. Hitler smelled an easy victory and immediately declared war against the U.S. America, still in shock, struggled as citizens rushed to enlist in the Army while the Japanese struck and conquered American and other western outposts in the Pacific.

My father had been a successful attorney. He did what he could before the attack on Pearl Harbor. He gave blood for the British who continued to fight and made donations. He took in German refugees on their way to South America and participated in other ways. The Japanese attack and subsequent declaration of war convinced him and my mother that he could do more and he shut down his law practice. He put our house up for sale and went to a recruiting center to enlist. By the end of December, he was in uniform.

The Army gave him a battery of tests which resulted in several options. They told him that he was qualified to be an officer, but at age 37, he was too old for many jobs, or he could receive a direct commission as a captain in the Judge Advocate General Corps (JAG) and become a lawyer in the Army. Another option was to enter OCS (Officer's Candidate School) and graduate as a second lieutenant, the most junior officer rank in one of the Army's many branches. He asked for OCS Infantry with his second choice in OCS Air Corps. He knew he was too old for pilot training. However, he had heard that other jobs involving flying might be open to candidates who were otherwise qualified. He was informed that to be an infantry officer, he was again too old. He finally settled on Air Corps OCS and while going through OCS he chose Air Intelligence Officer as a specialty.

All officers who were commissioned through OCS were known as "90-day wonders," as it only took ninety days of officer training as opposed to four years at West Point or ROTC at a civilian college or one year of flying training for pilots as aviation cadets who had two years of prior college education. He was in good company in OCS because officer candidates came from all professions and some were celebrities. One upperclassman in his OCS squadron of about 100 officer candidates was Clark Gable, a famous movie star of the day.

After graduating from OCS and until my father was eventually sent to a combat unit overseas, the social gatherings in the States were at the officers' clubs where married officers were permitted to take their families for meals and entertainment. I was six years old and hung out with the young pilots who were mostly in their teens. They allowed me to pester them with my many questions about flying and their training. I couldn't wait to grow up and join them.

By the end of the war in 1945, my father (and Clark Gable, too) had both flown in battle and reached the rank of major. My father left the Army and returned to practicing law as a civilian, and Clark Gable returned to making movies. However, my father found that he liked military life where, with the bad and the good, he was treated like everyone else and not singled out by society because he was Jewish. When offered the opportunity to return to the Army about a year after the war, this time as a JAG officer, he quickly accepted.

West Pointers were the at the top of pecking order among other officers in the military. Officers who had graduated from West Point were looked upon as special by the "90-day wonders." There was occasional jealousy of course, but also respect for a West Pointer's knowledge and professionalism and getting through what was known to be a demanding program of instruction.

My Limited Jewish Education

Unfortunately, the country was at war when my father started his service and I was five years old. There were 550,000 Jews serving in the Army, but rabbis were scarce. To get a military rabbi, or chaplain at any assignment, you had to have a minimum number of congregants. Most Jews were concentrated in the larger training bases. My father was generally assigned to smaller flying training bases and not near towns in which there were civilian temples and synagogues to attend. Therefore, my Jewish education was almost non-existent. Usually the Army made available a central location for several hundred for Passover services, and as a result this was usually the only Jewish holiday which was celebrated by my parents. After the war, things got a little better. My parents identified more with Reform, rather than Conservative or Orthodox Jews. In one city I received enough Jewish education from a Reform group to be "confirmed." However, upon becoming 13 years of age I never went through a full Bar Mitzvah or celebration thereof. When I went to West Point, I couldn't read Hebrew, nor did I know the prayers.

Getting Ready for West Point

I worked hard academically and physically to prepare myself and I read every book I could put my hands on about West Point. I knew that getting a West Point appointment would be tough both to win an appointment and tough to get through the West Point academic work and training. It was extremely competitive. Not only was it a topflight education with no tuition charges, but a cadet got paid to go there! How can you beat that! So, when I graduated West Point, with a little help from my dad I had enough money for my officer's uniforms and a down payment on a car.

Although all my friends before West Point were non-Jews, I was generally treated well in the military during my childhood and youth with rare exceptions. Anti-Semitic behavior in the military was strongly discouraged. It never came up at West Point after I was commissioned. I was able to easily handle the few incidences that occurred among a few ignorant fellow officers.

There were 550,000 Jews in the U.S. Army during WWII. We were still less than 3% of the U.S. population so the numbers serving at any single location were generally small. This included West Point. This had some implications.

50% Jews in the First West Point Class in 1802

The problem with small numbers of Jews meant that you wouldn't have an assigned rabbi to that location. You had to have a minimum number of congregants to get a military chaplain. The first class at West Point in 1802 was 50% Jewish! Unfortunately, there were only two cadets in that first class of 1802, and one was Jewish and one was not.

A century and a half later, in my class of 1959, the number of cadets had increased substantially, but Jewish percentages were much lower. There was a total of about forty Jews out of 2400 cadets. We still did not have enough Jewish congregants, so we had a volunteer civilian rabbi, Rabbi Kaplan, who served as our part time rabbi. He was a real blessing.

We didn't have a Jewish chapel when I was a cadet. The Catholics got their own Chapel in 1900 separate from the Old Cadet Chapel built in 1845. The new Cadet Chapel was built in 1910. No administration, Democrat or Republican in Washington could justify building a Jewish Chapel for use by only 40 cadets. Finally, the Army decided some years after I graduated that West Point was an important enough assignment that it should have a full time rabbi whether it had the minimum number of congregants according to Army regulations or not. I met several rabbis when visiting West Point over the years, and most were first rate.

Long after my time at West Point, Jewish alumni from around the country formed a chapel committee and raised the needed funds and in 1984 with the help of Jewish communities throughout the U.S., and encouragement by the West Point administration, a Jewish chapel was built without government funding. Prior to the Jewish chapel being built we used the Old Cadet Chapel for Jewish services with Christian symbols of worship removed and replaced by the Star of David and Menorah during Jewish religious services. It was thrilling to know that we sat and worshipped in the same places as the heroes who had gone before us Jewish and non-Jewish from 1845 on until the large new Cadet Chapel was built. Nowadays with our own Jewish Chapel I have worshipped there. I have also spoken there for my eldest son's Baccalaureate service when he graduated in the class of 1992, and for a Machal group from New York City celebrating the anniversary of those who volunteered to fight for the establishment of the State of Israel in 1948-49. Since 1802, more than a thousand Jews have graduated from West Point.

My Jewish Education at West Point

From 1955-1959, the four years I was a cadet, West Point was quite different from today. Attending religious Jewish services was not voluntary–it was mandatory! In fact, all religious services were mandatory. You had your choice–you could declare yourself a Protestant, a Catholic, or a Jew, but one of the three you must be! And you were required to attend religious services every Sunday morning at 0830. Yes, you heard it right, Sunday. There was no such thing as avoiding going to religious services because you were an agnostic or an atheist. And there were no Friday evening services. Every Sunday morning, we marched a mile or so to services and then marched back afterwards, and the other religious groups marched to their chapels at the same time. That was West Point thinking. Every cadet, who were all male cadets at the time, was treated exactly the same regardless of his background or religion.

Weekly Activities During New Cadet Barracks

During our first summer at West Point on Friday nights, we got together with the rabbi weekly during New Cadet barracks known as "Beast Barracks." For those of us who were Jewish, this was something special because the rabbi brought and set up lox and bagels for Oneg Shabatt. It only lasted about an hour, but it was most welcome because we were new cadets in training and the one-hour for Oneg was the only time we could socialize or even talk to a classmate publicly during this basic training. "Beast Barracks" was tough both physically and mentally and there was no orientation on entering the academy as there is today, or welcoming of parents at the time the new cadet entered West Point. In those days we weren't even allowed mail or to go to a public place the first month, even if we had a few hours free on the weekends. The Oneg provided a welcome break from a very difficult period of transition from civilian life, which otherwise didn't exist at West Point in the late 1950s.

My third year, I realized that I knew so little about Jews and Judaism. It was a little embarrassing that many of my non-Jewish classmates knew more than I did. It was that year that I met one of the most outstanding cadet leaders I had the privilege of meeting during my cadet tenure. He was the highest-ranking Jewish cadet during my third year and commanded the cadet company assigned right next to mine. He was two years ahead of me in the class of 1957. Wally was an unusual cadet in many ways. First, Wally was older. The maximum age to enter West Point was 22. I think about 20% of the cadets during my time had one or more years of college when they entered West Point. A few had actually graduated a four-year college. But Wally had done better than that. He had not only graduated from UCLA, but had been commissioned through ROTC and had served in the Army and reached the rank of 1st lieutenant, which is one rank higher than the rank you receive when you graduate West Point. He had given up his commission to attend West Point and started all over again.

Also, he was unique in that he was half Chinese, and his mother was Jewish either by birth or conversion, which, I don't know. He was given no special privileges as a former commissioned officer and had to take the same courses and go through the same training as everyone else.

In addition during my time at West Point, there was an annual Passover Service conducted at which guests and parents might attend. Either the Superintendent, the highest-ranking officer at West Point, or the Commandant, the second highest, attended the annual Passover Service. Neither was Jewish, but it was much like the military Passovers I attended during the war. Later, during the Vietnam War, I attended a Passover Service in Bangkok, Thailand when I was flying combat missions as an air commando over the jungles of North Vietnam and Laos.

Today at West Point, it is not mandatory to march to religious services or attend religious services Services are at the proper time according to your religious requirements. Muslim and other religious services are available and female cadets have been accepted since 1980.

My junior year was significant because it was the academic year. We labored under courses in electrical engineering and thermodynamics and were required to complete a nine-month study on some topic approved by one of our professors for sponsorship and guidance. I didn't encounter anything like it again for twenty years when I began my doctoral dissertation.

That same year as part of our curriculum, we were given one of our few "electives." Nowadays there are plenty, but in those years, there were very few. One elective at the time was an alternative to taking a single year-long course in European history. You exercised this "choice" by taking a test in European history which was optional. Of those who took the test the top 60 didn't have to take European history. Instead of this single year-long course, you took shorter courses in Russian, Chinese, and Middle Eastern history. I took the test, scored among the top 60 and it had an effect on my future, in a way which I could not have imagined.

Israel's 100 Hour War

The previous year in late October 1956, Israel, a tiny country that I had barely heard of pulled off an upset in the Middle East against a much larger and better equipped adversary repeating an unexpected victory against tremendous odds accomplished less than ten years earlier when Israel had won its independence and established itself as a State even though invaded by five enemy armies. Israel was populated by Jews, many of them survivors of the Holocaust in Hitler's attempt to annihilate all Jews. Israel's unexpected victory was discussed in every classroom. Jewish cadets now were looked at somewhat differently–not as belonging to a minority which was to be reassured that they would be treated as equals at West Point, but rather that as fellow cadets that might possess some unique knowledge or abilities which might be of use in the military profession.

A little less than a year later I began my middle eastern studies. My professor was Captain Charlie Simpson, an infantry officer who wore both parachute wings and a ranger tab. All of our professors had advanced degrees in their specialties. Captain Simpson had his from Harvard and had a distinguished career eventually retiring from the Army as a full colonel. I approached Captain Simpson and asked if I might do something having to do with Israel and asked if he would be my advisor. He was enthusiastic! I discovered that he had been on the Military Attaché's Staff in Israel and was keenly interested in anything I might propose. This got me started in hours of research at the West Point Library and other sources for a research paper on the development of the Israeli Army. In the process, I learned for the first time about Judaism, my own people and Israel in some detail. I became incensed with the injustice Jews had received over the millennia since Jerusalem was destroyed and we were enslaved by ancient Rome, and as in modern times had fought against superior numbers. Eventually, my marriage and what I learned of Jewish history at West Point led me to resign my commission in the U.S. Air Force. I joined the Israeli Air Force and participated in the Yom Kippur War. Then I rejoined the U.S. Air Force.

Although, I could never bring myself to have a Bar Mitzvah, after passing the designated age of manhood. Nevertheless, when we came to California, and I associated with Chabad, I at one time was fluent in Hebrew and learned the essential Jewish prayers so I could perform some of my duties as one of the *cohanim*.

About the Author

Major General William A. Cohen graduated from West Point in 1959 and was commissioned in the U.S. Air Force. He flew 3000 hours in B-52 nuclear bombers and was first in his class promoted to the rank of major. He was selected to attend the University of Chicago for an advanced degree for an assignment in research and development. However, on graduating he deferred his assignment and volunteered for the air commandos. He flew 174-night interdiction missions over the jungles of North Vietnam and Laos winning four Distinguished Flying Crosses and other decorations. Then he completed two years in research and development, left the US Air Force, and joined the Israeli Air Force fighting in the Yom Kippur War of 1973. He rejoined the US Air Force, earned a doctorate and rose to become a general while writing 60 books on management published in 25 languages. He cofounded a nonprofit graduate school after retirement. He was awarded the Distinguished Service Medal by the Air Force Chief of Staff and has received numerous other civilian and military awards.

Good Morning, God!

Helen Janiger

Good morning, God!

"Good morning, yet. You kept me up all night talking to me and now you wake me again! Such a 'nudnick'! Tell me, do I wake you from a sound sleep"?

Yes, God, You do. Sometimes Your light is so brilliant that it wakes me right up out of my complacency! But I'm not stingy! I adore You when You awaken me. I don't call You a nuisance! What are You for, if You can't be available to me? If you make Yourself inaccessible?

"What am I for? Where's the respect?"

I'd rather love You than respect You, God.

"So alright! You want to blame me, too, like everyone else? You forget who is God, me or You?"

Of course I know You are God and I am mortal. That's why I need You.

"And have I ever failed you? Tell me. Am I always there when you call me?"

Always, God. And I don't blame You for anything. But You made some strange mistakes when You created this universe!

"Who Me? God made mistakes? Such a thing! You are impertinent! Where do you get these ideas?"

They come when I'm afraid You will abandon me.

"Have I ever abandoned you? I ask you!"

No, You haven't...but why did You create human beings and then abandon them?

"Because I decided that I didn't want to be omnipotent or omniscient anymore. It's too much responsibility. Can't you understand that?"

Yes. I do understand. But look what happened! Left to it's own devices, mankind got itself into a miserable mess! Why couldn't You at least leave some light for them?

"What? The sun isn't good enough? And the moon is bad, too, I suppose? All that's necessary is to receive it, to become part of the light and then you are a part of me. Don't you understand that?"

I know, God. And that's when I know there is no way for You to abandon me. But there's so much I don't understand. I mean, what were You thinking of when You made a hippopotamus? I mean, that's really weird! And what could You possibly have in mind when You made us all predators, part of a pecking order? The very idea that creatures have to eat each other in order to survive! That's really not very nice! And the concepts of hell and sin and guilt! What a burden to put on us! How does such confusion serve You?

"Ah-hah! So you did wake me to complain, after all? You want my compassion and I'm supposed to give it to you whenever you like? Well, Mrs. Arrogant Helen, where's your compassion? Do you think you could do as well on your first try? Remember, I didn't have any experience, and just look at the universe that I made! Could you make a rose or a butterfly or a rainbow, Mrs. Inconsiderate? Or a light show like I give you every day in my ever-changing sky? So... what do you have to say for yourself? You think you could do it?"

No, God. Forgive me, please. I apologize. I would water plants and help them grow, but I can't create one. You are right, God, as always. I've created some strange worlds of my own and filled them with more ridiculous creatures than hippos. And do you know, god?

My creatures were always black and white. I didn't know how to give them shading or color. I'm sorry.

"Alright then. You're finally coming to your senses. Besides, I think I did pretty well, even with the blunders. I can admit my mistakes too, you know. I realize that I didn't do so well when I designed the human body. I've felt bad about that for millennia. But remember, I didn't have any directions or any one to teach me! So in light of that, I didn't do too badly, after all. And once it was done I couldn't correct the errors. I've always been sad about that. Once I gave life to everyone and everything, my work was done. I knew that I had to release the process of growth and development to all of my creatures, man and animals alike. I didn't realize that mankind would go berserk and race towards it's own destruction. Go now. I gave man a brain but it never occurred to me that it would be used so poorly. I thought that man would be my most civilized creature because of the brains I gifted him with. Instead, all of you went crazy! Who could think of such a thing on the first effort? I ask you. Madness was not in my plans, I'm supposed to know everything without any directions to follow? I was supposed to predict that human beings would learn to kill one another? Or, be so mindless that they created disease because of poor habits and bad sanitation, and then lay the blame at my door? And then I'm supposed to be available at any hour to clean up the mess? This aggravates me so much. Don't you people realize that I'm human too?"

Of course, God. I realize that. And I can see Your pain and it's heartbreaking to hear You speak as You are doing. Honestly I don't blame You and I never have. I love You deeply and I revere you profoundly. It's just that its been so hard to understand Your reasoning during those first seven days. Now I feel more clear about it: Thank You for telling me.

"That's better, Helen. Okay, now I can open my heart to you. Besides I didn't abandon your kind completely. Remember, I sent my Son to speak to you and show you the way, when I saw some of the mistakes I made. And it wasn't my fault that he was misunderstood by so many. Both of our hearts are broken about that and I don't want to be depressed about it any longer…"

Oh my God, God! Do you get depressed?

"So why not? You think I shouldn't feel bad about what happened? Don't you feel bad when you see your mistakes? So, why shouldn't I? But remember, I gave the miracle of life to everything and everyone. I gave the greatest power of all…the power to give birth. That gives me joy and hope! Who else do you know who could have such vision as mine? Who had enough imagination to create such a miracle?"

No one, God. Only You. That's why I love You so much.

"Alright! That's better. Now I will listen to you. Did you wake me just to remind me of my fallibility? Surely you had better reason than that."

Yes, God. I really want to tell you something quite different, something that's very important to me.

"So speak! Don't be shy."

I'm shy because I feel very tender and I want to be careful now.

"What about?"

About me and my dance. You see I'm learning to dance with two powerful partners. One is "Life" and the other one is "Death." And there are clear rules that must be obeyed by all three of us. You see "Life" and "Death" are permitted to cut in on each other at any time and the partner with whom I am dancing must release me without question or hesitation to the other partner…

"Yes. Go on."

Well, sometimes I feel like a ball that's being tossed back and forth by these two Giant Partners, and the wonderful thing is that I am learning how to bounce without hurting myself.

You see, God. I love them both, but sometimes I wish that I had some choice in the matter.

I think I'm more accustomed to "Life" as my partner. I trust him completely and I've come to learn that when I am in his arms there will be no more sudden shocks, even when he is capricious and chooses to go from the beauty of a waltz into the bedlam of acid rock. My feet have learned to follow and I am not alarmed. But I've come to know that when I dance with "Life" as my partner, I must be ever vigilant, ready always to change the rhythm without warning. That feels good to me. I know that I am fully capable of following the lead with "Life" without missing a beat. We've been dancing together for so long. But it requires constant and consistent awareness in order to keep my balance, and that is sometimes very tiring, especially when I am taking "chemo." And then there are the interruptions when "Death" cuts in without any concern at all about my partnership with "Life."

And I find "Death" seductive, indeed. His music is not familiar to me and I haven't learned any of the dance steps, but I know that I can relax in his powerful arms. I know that he will carry me wherever I am supposed to go. He requires nothing of me but trust. And I do trust him. Sometimes I even allow myself to be lulled into a velvet-quiet sleep. It feels so good, God! So good that I want to stay in his gentle embrace forever! And usually that's when "Life" cuts in to demand his turn with me. You see, he's just like "Death," he doesn't care at all about what we're doing together...and sometimes I feel pretty miffed at both of them for being so rude to each other and to me..."

"So, what happens then?"

Well You see, God, that's when I leave both of them to pout in order to listen to my own music. My music is a symphony played by a grand orchestra and You are the Conductor! You arrange the orchestration and the harmony! You create the concerto that transforms me! I can hear the celestial music and I am transported to realms beyond imagination…

"Yes. Go on."

There isn't any more.

"You awakened me to tell me that?"

No, God. I woke You so that I could thank You. You give me the instructions when I sleep and dream. You teach me how to dance in step, whether my partner is "Life" or "Death," it doesn't matter. I'm prepared to follow wherever I must go, even during those times when I must leave both "Life" and "Death" because I must be alone with You.

Well, I feel awkward. I'm only trying to thank You! To show You my deep gratitude. To let You now how much I love You and how safe I feel, no matter who cuts in! I love You, God! I love You with all my heart.

"I see. Thank you, my child. Now I understand. I'm happy that you awakened me to tell me this…and that you gave me the opportunity to speak of my sadness and you to you. We grow ever deeper. Now it's time for both of us to rest. But before we part, I bless you and tell you that I love you, as well. You are my child of innocence and I forgive your arrogance. You don't need to be pious when I feel your reverence. Go now and listen carefully to all of the music to which you must dance."

Thank You God. I will.

One Soul's Journey

Mary L. Marquez

"This is what you shall do: Love the earth and sun and the animals, despise riches, give alms to every one that asks, stand up for the stupid and crazy, devote your income and labor to others, hate tyrants, argue not concerning God, have patience and indulgence toward the people, take off your hat to nothing known or unknown or to any man or number of men, go freely with powerful uneducated persons and with the young and with the mothers of families, read these leaves in the open air every season of every year of your life, re-examine all you have been told at school or church or in any book, dismiss whatever insults your own soul, and your very flesh shall be a great poem and have the richest fluency not only in its words but in the silent lines of its lips and face and between the lashes of your eyes and in every motion and joint of your body." [1]

I started out on my journey to Judaism at a very early age. I asked too many questions and I did not understand why I had to go to catechism and memorize prayers which I did not understand and what they had to do with G-d. Nevertheless, I memorized them. Words were not enough. Anyone can memorize a prayer, but not everyone knows G-d. The concept of "G-d is everywhere" made sense to me because that G-d was not a man. G-d knew who I was and in my young mind, I began to ask a lot of questions. Who are you? Who is G-d? Why is G-d only important when someone is born, is married and dies? Where is G-d when there is not enough food to eat, space to grow, new clothes for school and unconditional love to give and take equally? Where?

As a child and growing up, in my home, there was not much time for reflection about anything. Especially, one's soul. Both of my parents were hard working people and in their own young selves did the best that they could do with who they were and what they had inherited. The work ethic was instilled in me by both word and example every day. Education was important, but only as it related to "Work" and of course money. However, I began my real education by observing what others did and listening to what others said, and once again, where was G-d?

When I was a young woman and worked my way through university, I observed and listened to my professors and fellow students. I studied Spanish literature, linguistics and English, Latin, French and German. What did I learn, besides languages? I learned that all people have a history, culture, religion (sometimes no religion) and trials and tribulations of every kind. I learned about persecution, slavery, exile and killing in the name of God and so many other Gods.

What I found most intriguing and knew so little about was that some of my ancestors from Spain had been persecuted, exiled and killed for being Jews. That fact did not make me feel any different from my Native American, Mexican-American, Portuguese, North African, Italian, and Greek ancestors. In other words, all of my ancestors had and have been humiliated, persecuted, forced into slavery, exiled and killed for millennia. This learning did not make me a better person, but it did give me a different perspective: an awakening to be present to my true self and to others.

In my quest for a framework to address my true identity: soul, I began to study other religions by simply reading about Buddhism, Christianity, Hinduism, and whatever other isms I could find. I even participated in various "faiths" to try them out. The meditations, prayers and rituals were very satisfactory for my soul at the time. But my soul had not yet landed. It was still flying looking for home. I didn't have to go too far to find it.

JEWISH MYSTICISM
Kabbalah: Receiving of Tradition from One's Past
The Journey of the Soul

"The purpose of the soul entering this body is to display her powers and actions in this world, for she needs an instrument. By descending to this world, she increases the flow of her power to guide the human being through the world. Thereby, she perfects herself above and below, attaining a higher state by being fulfilled in all dimensions. If she is not fulfilled both above and below, she is not complete.

Before descending to this world, the soul is emanated from the mystery of the highest level. While in this world, she is completed and fulfilled with the fullness of all worlds, the world above and the world below.

At first, before descending to this world, the soul is imperfect; she is lacking something. By descending to this world, she is perfected in every dimension."[2]

The question which I was truly asking myself was, how do I reach G-d directly. Although, I didn't have the words for it in my youth, I already knew the answer to that question. My soul was the answer. My soul was part of G-d. The invisible existed and my soul was the spark which belonged to me and the entire universe simultaneously: *emanation*.

I always felt the presence of G-d in the emanation experiences from childhood and my youth. In my beginning studies of Kabbalah, "receiving or that which has been received," I discovered that there was something much more than ideas or thinking in what most people know as soul; that which I could not see or name was real. Truly, I was returning to my *Serfardi* spiritual roots. I was also returning to my Native American spiritual roots some of which parallel Jewish Mysticism.

My initial Jewish Mysticism studies comprised of the *The Sefer Yetsirah* (Book of Creation), *The Sefer Ha-Zohar* (The Book of Radiance), which thereafter became the *Ha-Zohar Qadosh* (The Holy Zohar). It began as casual reading, but there was nothing casual about it. What a mass of concepts, methods and techniques of meditation (the 22 letters of the Hebrew alphabet and the archetype of the divine image: the 10 Sefirot). This "secret" knowledge was most certainly beyond my comprehension. Firstly, I did not read Hebrew, and I only read from translations. I have not stopped studying them. It will take a lifetime to comprehend them all. And I have accepted the fact that I may only understand very little even within my lifetime. However, there were glimpses of understanding, feeling and experiences which were familiar to me. For these glimpses, I thank all the Jewish mystics who by oral and written traditional studies over millennia explored and kept Kabbalah alive and well.

In studying Kabbalah, I had glimpses of a recognition of my soul.

Of particular interest to me there are the ten *Sefirot* or ten emanations: *Keter-Crown-Ayin* (nothingness), *Binah*-Understanding, *Hokhmah*-Wisdom, *Gevurah*-Power, *Chesed*-Love (loving kindness), *Tif'eret*-Beauty, *rahamim*-compassion, *Hod*-Splendor, *Netsah*-Eternity, *Yesod*-Foundation and finally *Shekhinah*-the Feminine aspect of G-d. According to Jewish mystical teachings, some mystics call it the Cosmic Tree of Life. I would call it the ten energy and spiritual aspects of G-d: the physical and the invisible simultaneously: *As above (the invisible) so below (the physical)*. For me on a very real level, I understand this to mean that as *a human being* I am not only a physical creature (below), but one that has another aspect which is that of soul which exists in what our senses cannot grasp because there is no name for it (as above; the invisible, the boundless, the Ayin or nothingness). And furthermore, what we do physically affects our soul and our soul is part of G-d. Soul is not an idea or thought, but it does exist. I do not profess that I understood or yet understand all this seemingly simple system of the ten Sefirot, or the methods and techniques of meditation utilizing the 22 letters of the Hebrew alphabet, but I do trust that my soul is part of that which cannot be measured and comes out of *Ayin* or *nothingness*.

Specifically, one of those glimpses in the recognition of soul was and is the Sefirah of "Tif'eret" which means *beauty*, or in Hebrew, *rahamim, compassion*. This recognition of *compassion* was something that I could easily identify with in my daily life. When I worked as a Vocational Rehabilitation Counselor for approximately 30 years, my occupation was not just counseling disabled workers, but having to stand in their shoes. I was a partner with them to evaluate, plan and counsel as to what kind of a future they might create for themselves in the world of work again. It was not just their livelihoods that I was dealing with, but the vulnerability of being human, the fear of the unknown and the on-going or momentary chaos in their daily lives. I was not paid for my compassion, but it was certainly necessary to make a difference in how they could perceive themselves as being fully worthy and productive human beings, and for me as well, because I loved my work and I was grateful for it.

My next soul recognition from Kabbalah, which was intertwined with "Tif'eret" was that of *tiquun* which in Hebrew means to *repair* or *mend*. My question in the context of daily life was to repair or mend what? The answer to that question was not so easy. If having compassion for another human being was a natural way of being for me, I knew that it was not always for other people. This made my work much more difficult in an arena where money was the first consideration for those disabled workers and for the payors of the services which I provided. In doing my counseling, I listened very carefully to each worker. I provided information and guidance so that they could help themselves (repair themselves) and in turn I received a lot of gratitude and in this way, I repaired myself, as well, by being able to accept their gratitude. In summary, what I realized and what made sense, was that whatever *tiquun* was to be done, whether physical or invisible, I realized and experienced that it would impact the lives of not just one, but the many. Therefore, it was not difficult to understand that what "I" do in this world does matter and does impact the whole of the community exponentially. In addition to that, I know that I am not alone in "doing" these repairs. My partnership in *tiquun* is with something much greater than myself.

There were many more awakenings to soul that I have experienced through the various studies in Kabbalah. The studies are not completed and I feel that I have just touched the surface. Although, aspects of Kabbalah are still a mystery to me, there is a clarity of practicality and pragmatism which pervades the teachings. No matter what challenges I have faced, I have persevered and survived into a continuing future which is now. Not only have I survived, but I have flourished. No longer are my prayers just rote recitation, but they are my heartfelt message *kavanah* in the "now" to G-d.

Ultimately, Jewish mysticism pointed the way to Torah. I went from these very specific teachings to Torah from whence those teachings originated. I discovered the *Mitzvot* or *commandments as* well as, *mitzvot* also meaning "good deeds" in Torah. Mitzvot as I understand them is the *doing* and *listening* part of our partnership with G-d. We do nothing alone. Mitzvot is what G-d wants us *to do*.

IMMERSION INTO TORAH AND LIVING BY CHOICE

> "The Sages teach that the Torah was available to every nation on earth, but no one would accept it. Bloody Edom could not accept a Torah that forbade bloodshed, thieving Ishmael wanted no part of a Torah that forbade stealing, licentious Moab could recognize no law without adultery, and so on" (Avodah Zarah 2b;Sifri; Brachah).[3]

Studying Torah was and still is an affirmation of my being human and having a choice of how to behave and live according to the *Mitzvot* which G-d offered to Israel at Sinai and which they accepted without doubt and enthusiastically: **"All that Hashem has said, we will do and we will listen."** (Exodus 24.7)

Immersion into studying basic Judaism and Torah, I became part of the Jewish community of faith. I had and have faith (trust) that what I was and am doing is beneficial for others, myself and with G-d. I learned by doing and listening and making friends. My friends were both Jews who had lived Judaism all their lives, those who were born a Jew and were learning about their faith, and those like myself, Jews by choice. Jewish services and continuing education were necessary and became a constant in my life. The most important services, which impacted my everyday life were Shabbat and High Holy Days. These were and are special days for directly connecting with G-d, not by oneself, but with community. Prayers during services were meaningful and elevating and joyful.

Furthermore, independent classes on specific topics presented by our rabbi were very interesting and expanded my understanding in how I was to be a Jew of faith. Many classes that I participated in were, of course relevant to liturgy and ritual and to specific scriptures from Torah. Still other classes were informal classes taught by rabbi in small discussion groups. One particular class which I remember was entitled "Lashon ha-ra". As I have studied and understand it, there is not a specific definition of this Hebrew term "Lashon ha-ra" in English. Literally it means "bad language" or "bad tongue". We discussed how words (bad language), negative words, or even true stories about others, gossip, tattling, lies and rumors impact another person's life. Anything said to lower the self-esteem of another person in order to elevate oneself, even if it is true, is considered Lashon ha-ra. Lashon ha-ra cannot be retracted and is hurtful to others. I found this type of class and learning very practical and applicable to daily life.

In summary, my continuing studies were fun, joyful and I made friends quickly. "Mitzvot" became a way of life. During one High

Holy Day preparation, I volunteered to prepare the Torah Crowns. I took a small toothbrush and cleaned them and polished them. I sat at a small table doing this for hours and though, it was not a great contribution, my rabbi said as he passed by, "Mitzvah" and he smiled. I will never forget his acknowledgement. It was complimentary and humbling at the same time. I knew at that moment that being a Jew of faith, would not be easy because I would never cease to learn something new and I was and would be learning with the Jewish community.

As Jews of faith, we are partners with G-d. We are not alone, but part of the concentric community, starting with the Jewish community and being part of all the communities in our country, all nations of the world and the universe. We are responsible for ourselves because G-d does not make money or pay our bills, or hand out miracles upon request. In being responsible, we strengthen our community and this impacts the collective consciousness of all souls. What we do and how we behave affects others. I remember recently, during High Holy Days, specifically, *Rosh Hashanah*, that my life partner was not able to attend services with me due to illness. I attended services alone or so I thought. As I stood up for prayer, and thinking that I was alone, I noticed rabbi's wife was next to me. I felt her presence as she placed her arm around me and we prayed together along with the rest of the congregation. At that moment, in prayer, my heart was full and I realized once again that our souls are boundless and that *Chesed* (loving kindness) is for everyone and it never has to end. And it doesn't.

It has now been twenty years since I made my affirmation and entered the eternal covenant between G-d and the Jewish people, the Children of Israel. I chose to become a Jew of my own free will. I accepted Judaism to the exclusion of all other religions, faiths and practices and pledged my loyalty to Judaism and the Jewish people under all circumstances…and I committed myself to the pursuit of Torah and Jewish knowledge. I was given the Hebrew name Rachel. My questions are continuously being answered and sometimes there are no answers. My soul found a home and I am still *doing* and *listening* now.

FOOTNOTES

1. Walt Whitman, *Leaves of Grass*, An Exact copy of Leaves of Grass, 1966. pp. v. & vii.
2. Moses de Leon, 13th Century, quote: "The Journey of the Soul", p. 148., Daniel C. Matt, *The Essential Kabbalah The Heart of Jewish Mysticism*.
3. (Avodah Zarah 2b; Sifri; Brachah), Talmud, quote: An Overview/ "Prelude to Sinai," p. xvi by Rabbi Nosson Scherman: *Aseres Hadibros The Ten Commandments/A New Translation with a Commentary Anthologized from Talmudic, Midrash and Rabbinic Sources*.

ACKNOWLEDGEMENTS
TO MY THREE TEACHERS

Rabbi Stephen J. Einstein, Temple B'nai Tzedek, Fountain Valley, California.

Thank you Rabbi Einstein for introducing me to Judaism in a most joyful manner and for embracing my interest in affirming and entering the eternal covenant between G-d and the Jewish people.

Rabbi Kenneth Ian Segel, Temple Sinai, Las Vegas, Nevada (2007-2009).

Thank you Rabbi Segel for your respect and sensitivity, and for acknowledging my interest and enthusiasm in participation at synagogue in whichever way I could contribute.

Rabbi Malcolm Cohen, Temple Sinai, Las Vegas, Nevada.

Thank you Rabbi Cohen for your acknowledgement of my service to temple, your refreshing and relevant classes, and sermons. FYI: I'm still working on my Hebrew. "I'm still working on it."

SUGGESTED READING

Cahill, Thomas, *The Gifts of the Jews How a Tribe of Desert Nomads Changed the Way Everyone Thinks and Feels*. New York, New York: Nan A. Talese/Anchor Books imprints of Doubleday a Division of Random House, Inc., paperback edition, 1999.

Feurer, Rabbi Avrohom Chaim, Translation and Commentary & An Overview/"Prelude to Sinai," by Rabbi Nosson Scherman, *ASERES HADIBROS/A New Translation with Commentary Anthologized from Talmudic, Midrashic, and Rabbinic Sources*. Brooklyn, New York: Mesorah Publications, Ltd , 1994.

Gerber, Jane S., *The Jews of Spain - A History of the Sephardic Experience*. New York, New York: The Free Press, First Paperback Edition, A Division of Simon & Schuster, Inc., 1994.

Kaplan, Aryeh, *Sefer Yetzirah The Book of Creation In Theory and Practice* Revised Edition. York Beach, ME: Samuel Weiser, Inc., 1997.

Kraemer, Joel L., *MAIMONIDES The Life and World of One of Civilization's Greatest Minds*. New York: Doubleday, 2008.

Kushner, Harold S., *The Lord is My Shepherd - The Healing Wisdom of the Twenty-Third Psalm*. New York: Anchor Books A Division of Random House, Inc., 2004.

Matt, Daniel C., *The Essential Kabbalah - The Heart of Jewish Mysticism*. New York: Harper San Francisco: Harper Collins Publishers, Inc., 1996.

Telushkin, Rabbi Joseph, *Words That Hurt Words That Heal - How to Choose Words Wisely and Well*. New York: Quill William Morrow, 1996.

Whitman, Walt, *Leaves of Grass*. An Exact Copy of the First Edition 1855 as Issued by Whitman and Received by Emerson. Brooklyn, New York: 1855. New York: The Eakins Press, 1966.

Wolf, Rabbi Laibl, *Practical Kabbalah A Guide to Jewish Wisdom for Everyday Life*. New York: Three Rivers Press, 1999.

TIKKUN OLAM:
Repair of the World
Adornment of the Mystery

Arthur Waskow

Being asked to explain my outlook on *tikkun olam* in 20 minutes is a little better–but not much–than being asked to explain the whole Torah while standing on one foot. I am therefore reminded of Shammai's response: to strike the questioner on the shoulder with a yardstick. For perhaps Shammai answered this way not out of anger but out of an earnest effort to do what the questioner asked, by responding in the manner of a Zen master. What is the Zen master trying to teach? That at the heart of the teaching is what cannot be taught; that at the heart of knowledge is what-cannot-be-known.

And this knowledge of the Mystery, of the limits on knowing, is I think, in our generation the most urgent thing to communicate to the world in our effort to "repair the world"–to do *tikkun olam*. In our generation, it seems to me, the two meanings of *tikkun olam* must fuse: the one expressed in the Alenu's L'teykan olam b'malkhut shaddai–"Repair the world through the Kingship of the All-nourishing"*–and in the mystics' use of "tikkun" to mean adornment, as when we adorn the Bride on Shavuot night, and their understanding of olam as connected with *ne'elam*, what is hidden and mysterious.

I do not believe that we will be able to preserve and renew our physical, knowable, livable world on the brink of total destruction–

unless we learn how to celebrate the Mystery–rather than pretend to Mastery. Unless we are able to say, *and to celebrate*, that we do not know what to do next. And to do this not only in the personal sphere of our individual lives but to do this in the public life of the community, the nation, and the human race. I would not have divided the "inner" and "outer" lives of the rabbi (or the Jew, or the human being) as our mandate did–for I think the real task is not to learn how to be "inner" in our "inner" lives and "outer" in our "outer" lives, but how to learn the rhythm of "inner-and-outer" in both the practice of the individual and the practice of the community.

Why do I think that the crucial wellspring of our political action must now be to say and celebrate that we do not know what to do? Because the human race is now so convinced that it knows what to do–that it is on the verge of doing itself in (and all of life besides). We have gotten so good at *doing*, that we have forgotten how to *be*; so good at *acting*, that we have forgotten how to *nurture*, so good at *making*, that we have forgotten how to *contemplate*: so adept at *mastery* that we scorn *mystery*.

And in all our frantic productivity, all our restless creativity, we face the urgent danger of the artist who is about to take a brush stroke too many–and thereby to finish off the painting instead of accepting that it is already finished. What is the artist's real task? To do no task. To pause and catch a breath–*shavat vayinafash*. *After* that breath, it will be possible to put a new canvas on the easel: to do another, different painting. But the picture we have been painting is finished. It was already finished before 1945–the inventions of the *kind* of efficient administrative organization and unifying propaganda that led to Auschwitz were already two brush-strokes too many–but must at least see how marred those strokes have made our painting, in order to learn that we must pause from doing new brush strokes of that same kind.

Yet we have in fact not yet paused to catch our breath. And it is only from pausing that we will learn what the new kind of picture ought to be.

The most urgent aspect of our world to which we must apply this form of *tikkun olam* is that of the H-bomb. The aspect of our lives in which the most profoundly important efforts are under way to remake the balance of *doing* and *being* is that of the relationship of women and men, "maleness" and "femaleness." I want to look at both of these.

First, the Bomb: the danger of a nuclear holocaust that could destroy all life. In the last three years, working on this question with groups of other Jews around *Menorah* and then through The Shalom Center I have learned how important it is to pause from our obsession with modern technical science and modern nationalist politics–and to reopen ourselves to the wisdom of the past, the wisdom that comes from before the human race got drunk on Torah. I have dealt elsewhere with the specifics of rethinking that have emerged, for example, from our wrestling with the Biblical tradition of the Flood and the Ark.** Here I want to underline that from our wrestling with these texts we reminded ourselves of the rhythms of life through time, the cycles of time for work and for rest. For the three great covenants of our tradition are all about these cycles: the Rainbow Sign, which comes to confirm that "seedtime and harvest, winter and summer, cold and heat, day and night: will never cease; *brit milah*, which comes to confirm by hallowing the (male) genitals that the generations will continue; Shabbat, the sign and symbol of the Sinai Covenant, which comes to confirm the spiral of work and rest which is at the heart of creation and all liberation.

For Shabbat is the sign, the symbol and the practice, of abandoning mastery in order to celebrate mystery. If we knew exactly what to do, Shabbat–not doing–would make no sense. If we knew that we could conquer our ignorance and learn exactly what to do,

Shabbat would make no sense. Shabbat only makes sense in order to recognize and celebrate that we *do not* and *cannot* know exactly what to do. That is the Mystery, not merely ignorance, that blocks our path to mastery.

What does it mean to apply these wisdoms to the prevention of nuclear holocaust? People say that *we do not know* how to end the arms race and make peace. I agree. We do not know. And *precisely* because we do not know, we should stop. That is the profound meaning beneath "the freeze." We should stop–and then we will discover, uncover, what to do next. Or rather it will be uncovered to us if we listen, watch, wait. Perhaps every seventh year–in a postmodern transcription of what it meant to let the land lie fallow every seventh year–we should pause in our technological research and development. Halt the engine that heats everything up, in order to contemplate and reevaluate.

And what does it mean to see the shift of power and practice between men and women in this light? I think that what is happening among women and men is a serious effort to rework the balance between nurturing and making things happen. In the modern world, the public sphere–the sphere of men–became obsessed with making and doing. Nurturing has been restricted, ghettoized, into the home–the sphere of women. (And even there it is being penetrated and swallowed up by the mechanized world of the media, etc.) So what is now happening is that women, who in their ghetto have learned to be experts at nurturing, are coming out of the ghetto–to insist that if the world is not to be destroyed, nurturing must become a *public*, not only a private practice. To do this effectively, women have had to learn to be effective–to be doers as well as nurturers. So to redress the balance in the world, women have had to remake the balance within themselves. And men–the experts in activism–have begun (only barely begun) to realize that *they must redress the balance within their own selves*, as well. They must learn to nurture–at home, and in the public arena.

This rebalancing is painful. The vision, dimly glimpsed, is to remake that original androgynous Adam who was split into "Man" and "Woman." The full and equal participation of women and men *and of women's and men's full life-experience* in all aspects of Jewish life and all aspects of human culture will mean more than equality; it will mean the transformation of Jewish and human culture. For us, it will mean the emergence of a new era of Judaism.

And this feminist or androgynist transformation of Judaism will be intertwined with the other aspect of our lives, in the development of a new–a "third"–era of Judaism. For the Jewish people, too, lives through great spirals of growth and transformation, work, and rest.

So now let me address what I think all this means to the great task of the Jewish people, to assist God in the making of *tikkun olam* in the sense of Alenu.

From the beginning and until the present, we thought of ourselves as a counter-culture. But we have done this work in basically different modes, during our two previous eras. In Biblical days, we thought of ourselves as an active, aggressive counter-culture resisting and trying to topple the Pharaohs, the Goliaths, the tyrannical and idolatrous Canaanite city-states, the Empires of the North. And the means we used–or at least the means we *said* we used–was chiefly violent and military. Then the Roman broke the back of our ability to do this, and dispersed our geographically united people– the basis for this military power–to the four winds. And we invented another way of being a counter-culture: dispersed, striving to be a model of decency and holiness that might be example–but certainly not by political power or assertiveness–help to transform the world. But *that* model received its death blow from the Nazi Holocaust.

And now? Beginning even before the Nazi Holocaust, but with absolute determination in its wake, we insisted on making ourselves politically powerful. And we have done so. Out of a small population and territory we built the militarily fourth most powerful state in the world. And in the *most* powerful society in the world–America–we build a sizeable amount of political clout–far beyond the proportion of our numbers. Even in the highly repressive society of the other super-power, the Soviet Union, we created the most troublesome and independent-minded sub-community.

But is that all there is to do? I do not think so. The political power we have built is modernist in form and tone–not Jewish in the sense of being rooted in our tradition, in wrestling with our tradition–and not spiritual in the sense of being rooted in Adornment of the Mystery. I think that in the era of the hypertrophy of war and the danger of world-wide nuclear holocaust, we need to achieve a new synthesis of the Biblical and Rabbinic modes. Our efforts at *tikkun olam* need to be assertive, outreaching, deliberate–as they were in Biblical days. The work of Gandhi and of King have shown us what is possible, but we should not forget the efforts of Shifra and Puah–the midwives who are described in Exodus as the first practitioners of non-violent civil disobedience. When Pharaoh ordered them to murder Israelite boy-babies, they did not respond by obeying Pharaoh–or my murdering them. They responded by choosing life and protecting life–and they initiated the movement that won our liberation.

It is not surprising, in the wake of the extreme suffering and victimization of the Holocaust, for us to think that there are only two choice: to be victims, or dominators. It is not surprising–but it is not correct. The kind of politics we need is a kind of Shabbat, a creative tzimtzum, in space and action. For this is what it means, when one has the power–to put boundaries and limits on it of one's free will. It is the unbounded expansion of our power to control that brings about our own destruction–and it is the ability to exercise self-control that gives our self its life and vigor in the world.

Let me give a specific example of what it would mean to act this way. Once upon a time, the shalosh regalism–the three "footmarch" festivals–were really marches, rallies, demonstrations. Hundreds of thousands of people came to Jerusalem in a manner demonstration numbers. But in Diaspora, we have celebrated these festivals–eaten our Sedarim, built our Sukkot–in our scattered homes and synagogues–in the nooks and crannies of the societies around us, not *en masse*. What would it mean now for us to gather again in thousands–at Pesach to oppose the Pharaohs who threaten to drown in Floods of Fire not only the boy-babies of our own people, but *all* the children of *all* the people? What would it mean to gather again in thousands, before the White House, the Soviet Embassy, a nuclear missile base–to build and live in the Sukkot Shalom that are open, vulnerable, leafy, light-filled inverse of a fallout shelter?

To reconstruct our peoplehood and our Torah in these ways will only be possible if we understand God in new ways. Not surrender God under the pressure of modernism, as many of us have done– and not cling to the King and Father of the past, as others of us have done. But to see God in each other's face, to see (as some of the Hasidim did) that Als iz Got: Everything is God. That in our era, God, so to speak, wants to be perceived as much more fully Immanent in the world, and has taken a major step toward *being* more fully immanent. That is why the human race now finds itself more possessed of, and by, powers that we once would have said were divine–the powers to destroy all life, to create new life, to overthrow a Pharaoh. The sense that God is Immanent in the world is not at all new to Jewish thought–as we know from reading the Songs of Songs and realizing that God is most present in the Song, *throughout* the Song, precisely because God's Name is never mentioned in the Song; as we know from the story of the rabbis' rejecting the Bat-Kol that spoke from Heaven, in favor of their own speaking of God's Word through their own decisions; as we know when we realize that the primal meaning of *YHVH* is simply the soul of a breath–y-h-v-h–and that the Siddur is trying to say this when it says that "*Nishmat kol chai tivarekh et shimcha:*" "The breath of all life blesses Your Name." But there is no doubt that behind the new powers of the human race there is a great new wave of Immanence. Part of the tikkun olam that we will need to do–in both senses, that of adorning the Mystery and that of repairing the world–will be remaking the ways in which we speak with the Immanent God: the ways in which we pray. As possibilities and examples: As do many havurot, we could davven in circles rather than rows, so that as we look for God we will indeed see each others' faces. We could use language like "Makor Ha-Olam." We could for *YHVH*, instead of saying *Adonai*, "Lord," either simply breath the breathy sound of "y-h-v-h" or say "Breath of Life" or "Yah." We could "embody" the words–make them immanent within our own bodies–by learning to use dance, mime, and body movement as part of our prayer. These too are part of tikkun olam, and they remind us that the distinctions between "inner" and "outer," "political" and "spiritual," are at best indistinct and at worst artificial.

I want to end by recalling one of the oldest moments of God's Covenant with what was not yet quite the People of Israel–and to see that moment in new light. Even before God gave Abraham the sign of the *brit* in circumcision, there was the overwhelming moment of the Covenant Between the Fires. And now, today, *We* are the generations that stand between the fires. Behind us are the fires of Auschwitz and of Hiroshima. Before us is the nightmare of the Flood of Fire–the thermonuclear holocaust that could burn the earth and make each city a crematorium without a chimney. The task for us is to turn fire into light: Light to see each other with, Light to see the Image of God in every human face. The task for us is to live between the fires of Shabbat: Behind us the candles that begin Shabbat; Before us the candles that end it with Havdalah. Within us the pause of rest, of peace, of mystery: Shabbat. We are the generation that must live between the fires: Between the candles of Shabbat, or the flames of holocaust. The flickering candle-flames of mystery, or the consuming flames of Mastery.

Blessed is the One Who creates from fire, *light*.

*This retranslation of "Shaddai" is based on the notion that it is rooted in "sheyd," breast.
**Arthur Waskow, "Interpreting the Flood Story in a Nuclear Age," Reconstructionist, February, 1984, p.11.

APPENDIX I
Brief Biographical Notes

William Alex, M.D. is an early (1953) graduate of the C.G. Jung Institute in Zurich, and has practiced for a number of years as an analyst in Los Angeles, San Francisco, and recently in Jerusalem, Israel, where his children have reached their maturity.

Rabbi Jack Bemporad, D.D. was born in Rome, was a Fullbright Scholar there and ordained at Hebrew Union College in 1959. He writes and teaches and is a Rabbi of Kehillath Israel in Pacific Palisades, California.

Robert Bosnack, J.D. is a Dutch Jungian Analyst, having graduated from the C.G. Jung Institute in Zurich. He practices in both Boston and Amsterdam.

Yishoel ben Baruch ha Chassid is a *nom de plume* for the world-famous *magus*, Francis Israel Regardie, D.C., Ph.D. Until his death in March 1985, Dr. Regardie was a leading exponent of the western occult tradition as carried by The Golden Dawn.

William A. Cohen, Major General USAF, Ret; Ph.D. See *About the Author* on page 215.

Gustav Driefuss, Ph.D. is from a very old Swiss Jewish family, and was originally trained in natural science. He graduated from the C.G. Jung Institute Zurich in 1959 and immediately emigrated to Israel, where he has been practicing ever since.

Rabbi Ted Falcon, Ph.D. is both a rabbi and clinical psychologist. He was ordained in 1968 at Hebrew Union College and earned a Ph.D. in 1975. He has lead his Synagogue for Jewish Meditation in the Los Angeles area, *Makom Ohr Shalom*, since 1976.

Helen Janiger has functioned as a non-titled psychotherapist for many years in the Los Angeles area, as well as a writer and mother.

James Kirsch, M.D. received his medical training in Germany and took his psychological apprenticeship with C.G. Jung. After considerable travels, he settled in Los Angeles and was a co-founder of various Jungian groups in the early 1940s. He continues to practice, write and teach in the Southern California area.

Mary Louise Marquez, B.A. in Spanish (emphasizing Linguistic Analysis, Literature, History and Culture) other language studies, English (2 years), French (3 years), German (3 years) and Latin (4 years) California State University, Fullerton, Vocational Rehabilitation Counselor/ Consultant & Work Evaluator California Workers' Compensation System, (1977-2007), National Rehabilitation Counseling Associate & Life Member, Founding President of Southern California Rehabilitation Exchange & Chair-Ethics Committee: Peer Review & Code of Ethics. Paralegal/Administrator and writer (2005-present).

Rabbi Levi Meier, Ph.D. was ordained as an Orthodox Rabbi, earned a Ph.D. in psychology at the University of Southern California and works as Chaplin (in both capacities) at the Cedar-Sinai Medical Center in Los Angeles, California.

Bertha Miller was a wife and mother until her death. She wrote the document contained herein, shortly before her death.

Martin Mondrus, M.F.A. is a Los Angeles artist who has taught for many years at Glendale College and has exhibited widely.

Gloria Orenstein, Ph.D. is Associate Professor of Comparative Literature and *The Program For The Study of Women and Men in Society* at the University of Southern California in Los Angeles.

Robert Rosen, M.D. is a physician, specializing in nephrology and "wellness" medicine. He is deeply committed to the Orthodox way of life. He received his medical training in California and Boston and currently resides and practices in Duncan Oklahoma. He was instrumental in the publication of the *Tanaya* in that area.

J. Marvin Spiegelman, Ph.D. is a clinical psychologist and Jungian analyst, having earned his Ph.D. in 1952 from UCLA and diploma from the C.G. Jung Institute Zurich in 1959. He lives in Los Angeles with his wife Ryma, where he practices, teaches and writes. His most noted books are *Buddhism and Jungian Psychology* co-authored with Mokusen Miyuki, Ph.D. and *The Tree*. Dr. Spiegelman is considered by many to be a world authority on psycho-mythology.

Daryl Temkin is a doctoral student in counselling psychology at the University of Southern California and interns at Cedars-Sinai Medical Center. He has studied Judaism in Israel and California.

Arthur Waskow is best known as editor of Menorah, a Jewish journal of renewal, and author of *These Holy Sparks: The Rebirth of the Jewish People* (Harper and Row, 1983). He also teaches at the Reconstructionist Rabbinical College.

Clara Zilberstein, Ph.D. is the daughter of many generations of rabbis, including her illustrious father, who was an outstanding personality in Los Angeles for many years. She is trained in Judaism and has also earned a Ph.D. in psychology.

New Falcon Publications
Publisher of Controversial Books and CDs
Invites You to Visit Our Website:
http://www.newfalcon.com

At the Falcon website you can:

- Browse the online catalog of all our great titles, including books by Robert Anton Wilson, Christopher S. Hyatt, Israel Regardie, Aleister Crowley, Timothy Leary, Osho, Lon Milo DuQuette and many more
- Find out what's available and what's out of stock
- Get special discounts
- Order our titles through our secure online server
- Find products not available anywhere else including:
    - One of a kind and limited availability products
    - Special packages
    - Special pricing
- And much, much more

Get online today at http://www.newfalcon.com